BALANCING A FULL PLATE OF RESPONSIBILITIES—FROM WORK TO HOME TO KIDS—CAN BE A HANDFUL

Add cooking three nutritious meals a day (plus snacks), and it can feel downright impossible. As a mother of three boys, Rachel Mansfield knows firsthand how important it is to find smart shortcuts without sacrificing flavor. She understands that every day can look different in a busy household. *More, Please!* is a survival guide for parents who need quick, reliable solutions for any time of the day.

Morning recipes such as HIGH-PROTEIN CINNAMON RAISIN QUICK BAGELS can double as snacks, while versatile bowls like CRISPY RICE BOWL WITH GINGER SESAME DRESSING help keep energy up all day. You'll find approachable fish options, including ONE-SKILLET LEMONY SHRIMP and SHRIMP & CORN CAKES WITH AVOCADO SALSA, craveable chicken dishes such as CHICKEN PARMESAN-STUFFED SWEET POTATOES, and various ground-meat recipes like tacos, meatballs, or casseroles. Enjoy low-effort sheet-pan meals like OUR GO-TO NACHO NIGHT NACHOS, including many ways to cook a box of pasta, like ONE-SKILLET CHEESY PIZZA MAC & CHEESE. Sweet tooth? Discover treats like SNEAKY GREEN SMOOTHIE PANCAKES and CHOCOLATE CHIP COOKIE CLUSTER GRANOLA that are so good you might eat them for breakfast, too. Plus, Rachel shares condiments, sauces, and sides to elevate your cooking with ease.

With family-approved, kid-friendly meals, freezable options, and dietary flexibility, *More, Please!* is the time-saving hack every parent needs to feel less overwhelmed. Because let's be real, no one has it all figured out. We're all just trying to get through the damn day.

More, Please!

More, Please!

FEEL-GOOD MEALS for BUSY FAMILIES and THEIR PICKY EATERS

RACHEL MANSFIELD

PHOTOGRAPHY BY
LAUREN VOLO

SIMON ELEMENT
New York
Amsterdam/Antwerp
London
Toronto
Sydney/Melbourne
New Delhi

For my three beautiful and perpetually hungry boys.

You fill my heart more than you'll ever know.
Being your mom is my favorite role in life,
and I cherish every moment of chaos in our kitchen.
This is all for you, boys.

CONTENTS

INTRODUCTION

More solutions, more ease, more enjoyment

Everyone knows feeding your family isn't easy. You've got a demanding job, countless household responsibilities, maybe a kid or two pulling at your leg, and frankly by the time dinner rolls around, some days the last place you want to be is in the kitchen.

Trust me, you're not alone! Social media makes it look like feeding a family is effortless for everyone but you. And more relaxing. And more delicious. And more glamorous. And as someone who literally creates food content for a living, I can tell you that it is . . . none of those things. Sure, it has moments that might *look* glamorous but often, preparing three nutritious meals—plus snacks!—every day for a family is, well, [whispers] kind of a pain in the ass. Not to mention, at this stage of my life I'm usually eating dinner cold (hello Bowls chapter!).

Enter *More, Please!* This is more than just a cookbook. It's a survival guide with tried-and-true recipes and tips from one busy parent or human to another. It's solidarity and encouragement that it's okay to take the shortcut, to let today be the rainy day and dip into your freezer meal stash, to pick one thing to actually "cook" and phone in the rest. It's a one-stop shop for making mealtime in your home *actually* effortless and, yes, enjoyable. You won't find elaborate date-night recipes or instructions for preparing a demi-glaze (I'm still not sure I know how to do that), but you'll find no shortage of recipes that feel beyond special and craveable enough to go on repeat for celebrations, holidays, and gatherings. The Pancake Trifle on page 45 is a family must-make!

The key to all of this? My years as a parent and a food content creator have taught me that the common thread to my (and your) favorite recipes is techniques and ingredients that are *repeatable* and *reliable.* For example, there's a reason I love meatballs so much: they take to pretty much any flavor combination, and any ground meat, and kids love them. There's a reason sheet pan meals are such a hit: it's mostly hands-off, you're dirtying one pan instead of like three, it lets flavors meld and come together so well, and it takes up less mental space managing the cooking process. Here, each chapter is basically built around a different repeatable, reliable main ingredient or kitchen tool (like our beloved sheet pans), plus some fun extras. You'll see a few familiar recipes in here, like my Cottage Cheese Pancakes, Thai Turkey Meatballs, and No-Boil Pasta Bake, because truly this book is not complete without the recipes that likely brought you to our family. These have been the viral, ride-or-die recipes that complete the book of "What does Rachel's family make again and again?"

One final note: I need you to remember that no one has everything together all the time. We're all just trying to get through the damn day. Even when you don't feel like you're doing your best, and you serve pancakes with bacon and a bowl of fruit for dinner (one of my favorites, tbh), just know that you are a queen.

Cooking in a New Chapter

A bit about me and how I cook

When I was growing up, my mom made dinner just about every night. You'll even see family stories and dinner table memories in some of these recipes. And as much as I learned from my mom (and mother-in-law!) about cooking for and feeding the people you love, I recognize that my life, and my time, as a parent looks very different.

Since my first cookbook, *Just the Good Stuff*, was published in 2020, what I cook, and who I cook for, has changed and evolved so much. I've had three beyond adorable and wild kids: Ezra, Brody, and Cooper. Yes, three boys—hungry ones who eat nonstop! (As in, I literally don't leave the house without at least three snacks for each.) Our dining table also includes my husband, Jordan, who has celiac, which means that all the meals that I prepare are gluten-free. (More on that later.) We're also blessed to have extended family nearby, so on any given day a grandparent or two, or my brother, might come through the garage door of our home, looking to eat and hang out. It's quite a village, and between the kids' school and activity schedules and my work schedule as a content creator, and CEO and cofounder of Cadootz, the next-generation kids' snack brand, and managing partner of our VC fund, grt sht ventures, I've had to find an approach to cooking that fits our busy lives.

I've always been a shortcut girlie, but I tend to stay away from "life hacks" and trends, instead looking to strategies that fit my actual, real life. So here are some of the imaginary cooking rules the internet has somehow created that I routinely break:

I do not cook every night of the week!

I cook about four, maybe five nights a week. When a kid has soccer or some other activity, they're having a grilled cheese from a lunch box in the back seat and I'm probably eating a bowl or salad of sorts in the front. (The Kinda Thai-ish Noodle Salad with Steak on page 56 is life!) It isn't glamorous, but dang, it's efficient! And weirdly, the kids think it's kind of an adventure? I'll take it. Another night is inevitably leftovers, or some mashup of leftovers. And then we might go out to someplace easy and casual about once a week. I try to avoid takeout at all costs, because somehow my kitchen is still a mess afterward? Make it make sense.

I'd rather meal *plan* than meal *prep*.

I'm a pantry staple girlie for life (you'll see!), and I like to plan based on what I have, rather than cook much ahead of time. Instead of meal prepping for hours on a Sunday, I use that day

to restock, reset, and plan for the week ahead. I get groceries; quickly prep some produce, like slice cucumbers and wash berries; and maybe make a couple of dishes, like our spatchcock chicken or some cottage cheese pancakes, to keep in the fridge. Then I map out what's for dinner each night and just make sure we're locked and loaded with snacks and whatever else we need to get through the busy week. Since I keep a variety of staples on hand (and yes, I made you a list!), from ground meat and frozen veggies in the freezer to canned tomatoes, pasta, and other grains in the pantry, I have the freedom to make nearly anything I'm feeling that week without locking myself into super-specific ingredients.

When dinner is served, we are all generally eating the same thing.

I don't believe in "kid food" in my house (okay, sure, there are boxes of mac and cheese for emergency dinner situations). In general, we all eat the same recipe when I cook, because everything I cook is tweakable for the other eaters in my household. When we have Parmesan-Crusted Chicken Nuggets (page 102), for example, I like to put those on a loaded salad of sorts, or my Evergreen Lemony Parmesan Kale Salad (page 59), but my kids like to dip them in one of the many condiments in the Basics chapter and have them with some oven-roasted broccoli. When we have Lentil Bolognese (page 139), we do a mix of pasta and zucchini noodles. And then there are the nights I'll do taco bars, DIY bowls, or sandwiches-that-can-be-burgers-that-can-be-lettuce-wraps. In every recipe in this book, there's a flexible element that lets you pivot based on what makes everyone happy, without making two or three separate meals.

Some Thoughts on Side Dishes

This cookbook is a little unique in that sides aren't a huge part of it, because I crafted the recipes to minimize having to think about too many different meal components at once. As a result, we've got a ton of one-pot and sheet pan meals that cover all your nutritional bases, plus a seriously solid collection of proteins, grains, and greens that mix and match incredibly well. For the times you want an extra veg, or green, or grain, and you want to basically be able to make it in your sleep after reading the recipe once, here are some of my tried-and-trues:

- **Evergreen Lemony Parmesan Kale Salad** *(page 59)*
- **Chop-Chop Greek Salad** *(page 63)*
- **The Most Underrated Nourishing Lentil Rice Bowls** *(page 67)*
- **Any crisp lettuce with A Bit Lighter Greek Yogurt Caesar Dressing** *(page 228)* **or Too-Easy-Not-to-Make-Ranch** *(page 228)*
- **Better than Fresh, Frozen Broccoli in the Oven** *(page 221)* **(this saves lives, I'm serious)**
- **My Go-To Japanese Sweet Potato Wedges** *(page 217)*

- **My Tried & True Rice** *(page 213)*
- **No-Fryer-Added French Fries** *(page 218)*
- **Fluffy Quinoa with a Protein Boost** *(page 210)*
- **2-for-1 Herby Rice** *(page 214)*

My goal in writing this book is for you to be able to open it up on any night of the week and find something that a) sounds good and b) you've got most, if not all, of the ingredients for. Many of the recipes are truly one-stop shops, where you've got protein, vegetables, and a starch all in one dish. For the rest, I've included some suggestions for easy sides (also in the book) for mixing and matching. When it comes to feeding your family, there are no wrong decisions, but I hope this book makes that mealtime decision-making a little easier and more enjoyable! And who knows, maybe you will even crave cooking now?! Perhaps even your kids will want to help. My kids love a good five-minute assistant role!

A Quick Note about Gluten-Free Cooking

Why cooking gluten-free matters to me, but doesn't have to matter to you in order to love using this book

Jordan and I met in college, when we were both nineteen (babies!) at the same keg crawl. My first words to him—brace yourself for romance—were, "Is there more beer in the fridge behind you?" Something must have been in the air, though, because we've been together ever since.

Over the years, we've been through losses and wins, moves and kids, and nearly a decade ago, a celiac diagnosis. This means we've almost had more gluten-free years together than not, so paying attention to ingredients (gluten or otherwise) has pretty much always shaped how I cook as an adult. While it might seem to some like a devastating limitation, I actually think learning about what different ingredients do in order to make gluten-free versions of favorite recipes has been a gift. It means I know where gluten might be hiding in a familiar recipe, and maybe more importantly, what components are flexible—which, honestly, is most of them!

So when you look at these recipes and think, "Hmm, okay, this looks very tasty and familiar and not weird cardboard gluten-free food," it's because the gluten-free food we are cooking here is actually no more complicated than food cooked any other way. Sure, some of the flours you buy might be different (more on that in the next section), but the moves in the kitchen are the same.

All that being said, I didn't sell this book first and foremost as a gluten-free cookbook. I sold it as a cookbook for busy families who still want to eat together most nights, and eat nourishing and fun food when they do it. Accessibility was, and is, the most important thing about these recipes, which means *they all work* with whatever flour, breadcrumbs, or pasta you want to use. Bottom line: If gluten-free isn't important to you, use your all-purpose flour, your regular pasta, and the other ingredients you like. The end result will still be delicious, and the dish will be one you'll want to make again and again.

How to Use This Book

You'll find that this book isn't organized in a traditional way—no breakfast-lunch-dinner; no appetizer-soup-salad-main—because let's be real, that's not how our lives usually look. This book is made to be a workhorse and a right-hand companion, promising that no matter which chapter you open up to, you'll find quick, reliable, and craveable recipes for any time of day, and any day of the week, from an average Tuesday night to a birthday brunch. Here's a breakdown of what you'll find in each chapter.

Become a Morning Person

I feel like breakfast gets a weird rep: it's either something quick but that may not hit all the bases, or requires time standing over the stove on a weekday morning just to make something nourishing. This chapter proves you can have both quick and nourishing, with go-to recipes that aren't just for breakfast, but are also amazing for snacks, celebrations, or breakfast for dinner. I think of all the chapters in this book, this chapter also has the most freezer-friendly recipes, which ups the convenience factor even more.

Craveable Salads & Bowls

Okay, you might be asking: Why is there a salad chapter in a family-friendly cookbook? I'll tell you why. Because even if kids don't like salad right now, it doesn't mean they never will! As a parent, I want salad—and big bowls filled with veggies and grains and protein—to be familiar, and I expose my kids to it over time. I also like to make one dinner for my family, so if that means my husband and I can get our greens in, and our kids are eating just the chicken, or some plain lettuce, or a grain, that's cool with me! These recipes are also the MVPs of portability, and what I tend to bring with me in the car for dinner on the go.

Yes, You Can Cook Fish

Fish can be an intimidating protein source, and for that reason, I think a lot of people feel they don't cook it often enough. I readily admit I am one of those people! But these fish dishes are ones I *actually* make in my house, and I'd argue they're the least "fishy" fish recipes you can make. They're more interesting than just throwing a fillet in a pan, yet super approachable for any night of the week. And these are all fish varieties you can find at your local grocery store, nothing fancy or specialty.

Not-So-Boring Chicken

True confession: I hated chicken until about my mid-twenties. The reason? Turns out I wasn't preparing it the right way. The reason I didn't like chicken for so many years is probably the same reason people think chicken is boring: the flavor is pretty mild and so it can end up bland,

and the texture can turn out dry (the bane of my existence is a dry chicken breast!). But I've learned over the years that there's so much you can do to keep it moist, flavorful, and delicious, and I share the secrets in this chapter.

What to Do with a Pound of Ground Meat

There's a reason this is a ground *meat* chapter, because although ground beef tends to be the most popular, ground meat in general is so incredibly convenient and versatile. So, say you don't eat beef, but you have ground chicken. You can swap that in for any of the recipes in this chapter; they all work with whatever you have! Ground meat is also the backup option in my kitchen: I always, *always* have some in my freezer, so if it feels like we're low on everything else, ground meat is there to save the day.

What to Make with a Box of Pasta

Listen, there's a reason that pasta + jarred marinara + grated Parm is a classic family meal: everyone likes it and it's convenient to make. But the recipes in this chapter really take a humble box of pasta to the next level without requiring more work than that classic combo. Pasta always seems to be a "safe food" for a lot of kids, and often I'll have my pickiest eater choose his favorite shape of pasta and go from there. Even making that small choice gives kids a bit of confidence in the kitchen, even if they're not helping you cook. And just like in the other chapters, the shape of the pasta generally doesn't matter, so use what you have!

Sheet Pan Meals We All Need in Our Lives

I think a lot of people assume sheet pans are just for roasted veggies or chicken, but in this chapter we do sheet pan nachos, a stir-fry (yes, I get it's not technically a stir-fry but listen, the vibes are there!), and a chicken Parm that will spoil you for all other versions. I turn to these meals when I want a one-stop shop and don't want to dirty a bunch of pots or pans. Personally, I also think this chapter is the most versatile, using a range of different proteins from sausage to salmon, and packing in veggies with every meal.

The Dessert Stash

For me, a meal isn't complete without a little something sweet afterward. These desserts are my ride-or-dies; you'll find at least one or two of them knocking around my fridge or freezer at any given time. The best part? These are desserts for the non-bakers! Nothing fussy or advanced, so even if you don't identify as a baking person, you'll totally nail these and make them again and again. ***Hot tip:*** Many of the recipes in this chapter aren't just for dessert! We eat the oatmeal raisin cookies for breakfast all the time.

Not-So-Basic Basics & Staples

Believe it or not, this chapter was not part of the original plan for the book. But the more this book came to life, the more I realized I needed to share these easy, back-pocket condiments, sauces, and sides because they're really the backbone of how I cook. These are the recipes I rely on every single day, and the ones you'll probably memorize first and turn to most often.

Safe Swaps

Make it work for you!

As I mentioned, even though the recipes in this book can all be made gluten-free, they can also all be made with traditional flours, pastas, and so on. And speaking of flours, I'm gonna call for only two main types of flour in this book. That's it! Not that you can't use more, but I also don't want you to run out and buy a zillion specialty flours just so you can make what's in here. Who has the time? (Plus, some of those flours can be expensive!)

I also will often use coconut milk instead of cream for creamy dishes to lighten them up a bit, not because we're avoiding dairy (flip through and you'll see we're using *plenty* of cheese). Same with coconut sugar, maple syrup, and honey: I like to mix it up with these because I tend to avoid overly refined sugars, but it doesn't mean you're locked into them.

My main goal in this book is to make YOUR life easier in the kitchen. I trust you to use ingredients you think would work, especially with the recipes in here, because they were made to be flexible. If you shop through the Pantry Staples section (page 26), you should be able to make any recipe in this book!

Below are all the ways you can swap in and out for ingredients you like or have on hand.

GLUTEN FREE-FRIENDLY • You are going to notice that I label my recipes as either gluten-free, nut-free and dairy-free. Then some say "friendly" afterward some of those labels. The beauty of more, please is that this book is "friendly" for all dietary preferences and allergies. Can't eat gluten but want to make the pastas? Use your go-to gluten-free pasta. Can't eat dairy but there is cheese in a recipe? Omit it or sub a dairy-free alternative. And allergic to nut butter? Sub tahini and so on. You get the point. I created this book to be friendly and convenient for all.

Flours, Starches & Pastas

FOR BAKING

- gluten-free flour (make sure it has xanthan gum) ↔ all-purpose flour

FOR BREADING/DREDGING

- almond flour ↔ all-purpose flour ↔ breadcrumbs (you'll see plenty of baked goods with almond flour in this book, too!)
- Tapioca or arrowroot starch ↔ cornstarch
- Gluten-free pasta ↔ regular pasta ↔ chickpea pasta if that's your thing! Just note that gluten-free pasta tends to absorb more liquid as it cooks, and most of these recipes will remind you to add more liquid if needed.

Milk, Cream & Dairy

- Full-fat coconut milk ↔ heavy cream
- Plain Greek yogurt ↔ plain coconut yogurt ↔ plain (non-Greek) dairy yogurt
- Whole dairy milk (or 2%, 1%, or skim) ↔ unsweetened nondairy milk

Sweet Stuff

- Maple syrup ↔ honey
- Coconut sugar ↔ granulated white sugar ↔ brown sugar (if you like that flavor)
- Any mix-ins for baked goods are fair game! Chocolate chips, white chocolate chips, cacao nibs, frozen blueberries, sprinkles, butterscotch chips, the list goes on. It's your call!

Oils & Fats

- Avocado oil ↔ extra-virgin olive oil ↔ coconut oil (Note that coconut oil can give a coconutty flavor, which sometimes can be a good thing! Coconut oil is also usually more sensitive to heat, and can solidify quickly when introduced to something cold, like in a baking recipe, so just be on the lookout for that. I buy liquid coconut oil for those occasions.)
- Dairy butter ↔ nondairy/vegan butter
- Peanut butter ↔ any nut or seed butter such as almond, tahini, or sunflower butter

Sauces & Broths

- Chicken bone broth ↔ regular chicken broth ↔ vegetable broth ↔ water (I just like the extra protein in bone broth.)
- Coconut aminos ↔ soy sauce (The only difference is that coco aminos can veer a tad sweet, and soy sauce is saltier.)

Proteins

As you use this book, please be confident that in most cases, you can swap in any preferred protein (including tofu!) in nearly any recipe. Yes, we've got a chapter dedicated to chicken, and one to fish and seafood, because the former seems to have a reputation for being boring and the latter, a reputation for being hard to cook well. Just keep in mind that the cook time will likely vary. But I've made the Thai-ish Noodle Salad (page 56) with shrimp instead of steak (amazing); you can crisp up crumbled firm tofu for something like the One-Pot Creamy Mushroom Chicken and Rice (page 99); and I feel like doing the Mediterranean-Style Stuffed Salmon (page 87) treatment on a chicken breast would be incredible.

Back Seat Cheat Sheet

Okay, so, what's in that pre- or post-activity bento box that won't make an epic mess in the back seat?

We eat at home most nights, but inevitably someone's got soccer practice or karate or Little League, and my kids have come to love the adventure of packing a dinner to eat in the car. Another reason I think you'll love the recipes in this book is that so many of them are so easy to eat at room temp, reheat easily, or are finger foods, or all of the above! A good half of my kids' on-the-go favorites are recipes from this book, and the rest are easy things I can throw together quickly. And all of my faves are recipes you can find in ***More, Please!*** If your life looks anything like mine, check out the ideas below. Plus, no one wants their kids to load up on snacks in the car, then have zero desire for dinner when they get home. So, I hope this tip brings a little ease to the carpool craziness. Don't have time to prep a bento box every day? Same: That's what the Shake Shacks of the world are for.

10 Ideas for On-the-Go Kid Dinners

RECIPE	PAIR WITH	BONUS
Pizza quesadillas: your favorite tortilla, sauce, cheese, pepperoni	Frozen peas (they thaw quickly right in the lunch box)	Fresh fruit slices, veggies of choice, pitted olives
Chicken grilled cheese sandwiches: buttered bread, cheddar cheese (I love adding shredded chicken here for more protein.)	Raw veggies (like cucumbers, carrots, and maybe even some olives!) Too-Easy-Not-to-Make Ranch Dressing (page 228) for dipping	Crispy-Crunchy-Nutty Balls (page 186)
Greek-style quesadillas: think tortillas, feta cheese, shredded chicken, chopped tomatoes, chopped pitted olives, spinach (omit if green food isn't the vibe)	Fresh fruit or raw veggies. Creamy, Better-than-Store-Bought Hummus for dipping (page 222)	Crispy-Chewy Oatmeal Raisin Cookies (page 198)

RECIPE	PAIR WITH	BONUS
Cottage Cheese Pancakes (page 49) or **Sneaky Green Smoothie Pancakes** (page 37): (I love to make mini versions to tuck into lunch boxes!) I put a splash of maple syrup in those mini stainless-steel sauce containers I share on IG.	Cooked turkey or pork bacon or sausage (My kids are weirdly obsessed with eating it cold.)	Fresh fruit slices or veggies of choice
Tacos: warmed hard- or soft-shell tortillas filled with cooked ground taco meat and shredded cheese	Better than Fresh, Frozen Broccoli in the Oven (page 221)	Super-Quick Guacamole (page 64)
Homemade pizza bagels: Use frozen bagels or English muffins and warm them in oven with sauce and mozzarella cheese on top.	Fresh fruit or veggies of choice	Pepperoni or mini meat stick
Chicken and cheese taquitos: flour tortillas filled with cheese and shredded chicken, and crisped over skillet	Sliced carrot sticks with dip	Super-Quick Guacamole (page 64) or store-bought salsa
Turkey-cheddar pinwheel wraps: flour tortillas with roasted turkey slices, cheese, and any other mix-ins you want. Roll up tightly and slice.	Sliced cucumbers or desired veggies	Dressing or condiment for dipping
Chicken nuggets: either my Parmesan-Crusted Chicken Nuggets (page 102) or store-bought	Frozen fries or my No-Fryer-Added French Fries (page 218) with DIY Ketchup (page 225)	The Perfect Gluten-Free Chocolate Chip Cookie (page 193)
Tuna patty melts: go-to bread with tuna salad, cheese, and sliced tomatoes, sandwiched and cooked in the oven or stovetop	Fresh fruit or veggies of choice	Mini muffins (page 53)

HOT TIP

Buy a separate bento box, or whatever reusable, portable meal containers you love, to use specifically for dinners. Sound weird? Get this: My kids were calling me out on using lunch boxes for dinners (kids, so literal), so we ordered "dinner boxes" that, yes, are just another type of bento box that we just use for dinner on the go!

10 Meals I Take On the Go for Myself

Inevitably these are leftovers that I'll pack away for myself and either reheat quickly before we head out, or eat cold.

1

Chop-Chop Greek Salad with Za'atar Chicken *(page 63)*

4

Protein-Boosted Veggie Quinoa Fried Rice *(page 68)*

5

Crispy Rice Bowls with Ginger Sesame Dressing *(page 71)*

8

Italian Pasta Salad *(page 144)*

9

Garlicky Broccoli & Steak Lo Mein *(page 143)*

2

At-Home Chipotle-Style Chicken Burrito Bowls *(page 64)*

3

The Most Underrated Nourishing Lentil Rice Bowls *(page 67)* with any leftover protein on top

6

Fully Loaded BLT Salad *(page 72)* with some crackers on the side, or made into a sandwich

7

20-Minute Quicker-than-Takeout Shrimp Teriyaki *(page 76)*

10

Kinda Thai-ish Noodle Salad with Steak *(page 56)*

My Pantry *(and Fridge, and Freezer)* Staples

I've said it before and I'll say it again: My goal for this book is for you to be able to make a meal with minimal fuss, and without a special trip to the grocery store. I tend to shop once a week, and the majority of what I buy is the same thing, week after week! This list is my holy grail of anything and everything I like to keep on hand to make all of the family favorites in this book. If you shop through this (and let's be real, you probably have at least half of these already in your kitchen), you'll be good to go!

Cooking/Baking

Almond extract

Almond flour

Baking powder

Baking soda

Basmati rice

Cacao powder

Canned beans, especially chickpeas and black beans

Canned crushed tomatoes

Canned green chilies

Chia seeds

Chopped nuts, such as pecans, almonds, walnuts, and cashews

Creamy nut or seed butter, such as peanut butter, almond butter, and tahini

Dark chocolate chips

Dark raisins

Dry green lentils

Flax seeds

Full-fat canned coconut milk

Gluten-free all-purpose flour (with xanthan gum) or all-purpose flour

Kalamata olives

Low-sodium bone broth, both chicken and beef

Marinara sauce

Oat flour

Pasta, especially spaghetti, orzo, and lasagna noodles

Quinoa

Red curry paste (watch the spice level!)

Roasted red peppers

Rolled/old-fashioned oats

Salsa

Sea salt crackers (I am biased to cadootz!, of course)

Tapioca flour or arrowroot flour

Tomato paste

Tortilla chips

Tortillas (flour or gluten-free alternative)

Vanilla extract

Sweeteners

Coconut sugar

Honey

Maple syrup

Oils/Fats/Vinegars/Condiments

Apple cider vinegar

Avocado oil

Balsamic vinegar

Barbecue sauce

Coconut oil

Cooking spray (I like avocado oil)

Dijon mustard

Extra-virgin olive oil

Ketchup

Mayonnaise

Rice wine vinegar

Sesame oil

Sweet pickle relish

Unsalted butter

White wine vinegar

Whole-grain mustard

Fish

Canned tuna

Cod

Salmon (I love Alaskan king salmon when possible)

Shrimp

Veggie Rotation

Baby arugula

Baby spinach (fresh and/or frozen)

Bell peppers

Butter lettuce

Cabbage

Carrots

Celery

Cherry tomatoes

Frozen broccoli

Frozen corn

Frozen edamame

Frozen green peas

Garlic

Japanese sweet potatoes

Red onions

Romaine lettuce

Russet potatoes

Scallions

Seedless Persian cucumbers

Shallots

Snow peas

Spaghetti squash

Sweet potatoes

Tuscan kale

Yellow onions

Yukon gold or yellow potatoes

Zucchini

The Usual Fruits

Apples

Avocados

Bananas

Berries (fresh and/or frozen)

Lemons

Limes

Pretty Basic Spices & Herbs

Black pepper (pre-ground or in a grinder)

Dried oregano

Fresh chives

Fresh cilantro

Fresh dill

Fresh ginger root

Fresh parsley

Garlic powder

Ground cinnamon

Ground ginger

Italian seasoning

Kosher salt

Onion powder

Smoked paprika

Za'atar

Meat (aka the majority of our freezer)

Bacon (turkey or pork)

Chicken breasts

Chicken thighs

Ground beef

Ground chicken

Ground lamb

Ground turkey

Italian sausage

Skirt steak

Whole chicken

Dairy

Cheddar cheese

Cottage cheese

Cream cheese

Eggs

Feta cheese

Greek yogurt

Milk

Mozzarella cheese

Parmesan cheese

Ricotta cheese

BECOME A MORNING

PERSON

Dad-Approved Crumb Cake

FREEZER-FRIENDLY

SERVES 9

Gluten free
Dairy free

When I was a kid, I went to a friend's beach house and came downstairs in the morning to this amazing thing called crumb cake (which I had never seen before). I came home telling my parents all about it, and my dad—who is very health-conscious but also has a raging sweet tooth—confessed that even though crumb cake wasn't a breakfast thing in our house, it was one of his favorite things. So eventually, I figured out how to make it, and have made it for him for years. The texture of this cake is incredible, especially when you consider that it's gluten-free! It's great for breakfast, of course, but also makes a great afternoon treat with a cup of coffee or tea.

CAKE

- 1 cup unsweetened applesauce
- ½ cup coconut sugar
- ⅓ cup liquid coconut oil
- 2 large eggs
- 1 teaspoon vanilla extract
- 2 cups almond flour
- ½ cup tapioca or arrowroot flour
- 2 teaspoons baking powder
- 2 teaspoons ground cinnamon
- ¼ teaspoon kosher salt

CRUMB TOPPING

- ½ cup plus 2 tablespoons almond flour
- 2 tablespoons liquid coconut oil
- 2 tablespoons coconut sugar
- 1 teaspoon ground cinnamon
- Powdered sugar, for serving (optional)

MAKE THE CAKE: Preheat the oven to 350°F. Line an 8x8-inch metal baking pan with parchment paper and set aside. (You can use a glass dish if that's what you have, just note that the cake will take longer to bake.)

In a large bowl, whisk together the **applesauce**, **coconut sugar**, **coconut oil**, **eggs**, and **vanilla** until smooth. Add the **almond flour**, **tapioca flour**, **baking powder**, **cinnamon**, and **salt** and whisk again until smooth. Pour the mixture into the prepared baking pan and set aside.

MAKE THE CRUMB TOPPING: In a small bowl, add the **almond flour**, **coconut oil**, **coconut sugar**, and **cinnamon** and mix well to combine. Sprinkle the mixture evenly over the cake batter. Bake the cake until a cake tester or toothpick comes out clean, 35 to 40 minutes.

Let cool for a few minutes before slicing and serving. If you're feeling fancy, top this with **powdered sugar**!

SAFE SWAP

Not into coconut oil? Avocado oil is a great option with a more neutral flavor.

A NOTE ON SUGAR!

I've been using coconut sugar as a go-to sweetener for over a decade. I like it because it's less refined than white sugar, and it doesn't spike your blood sugar as much. If that's important to you, coconut sugar is easy to find in nearly every supermarket, as well as online. But if not, that's cool too! Swap in the same amount of granulated sugar for any recipe in this book that calls for coconut sugar.

Chocolate Chip Cookie Cluster Granola

MAKES ABOUT 6 CUPS

Gluten free
Dairy free

FREEZER-FRIENDLY

Okay, it's me: I'm the a**hole who buys a bag of granola, eats all the clusters, then moves on to the next bag. Granola is absolutely one of my desert-island foods, so I'm constantly making different versions. I've been making this one for almost ten years as a basic chocolate chip granola, but recently got inspired to try to steer it more toward a cookie vibe. Turns out, almond extract is that magic *something* that really creates a cookie flavor! Now, if you don't have almond extract, you can certainly skip it and the granola will be just as good. *Hot tip:* I store my granola in the fridge or freezer so it stays super crunchy. You have to try it!

⅓ cup coconut sugar

⅓ cup maple syrup

⅓ cup liquid coconut oil

2 tablespoons hot water

2 teaspoons vanilla extract

1 teaspoon almond extract

3 cups old-fashioned or quick oats

½ cup unsweetened shredded coconut

½ cup chopped pecans or walnuts

¼ cup flaxseed meal

3 tablespoons chia seeds

1 teaspoon ground cinnamon

½ teaspoon kosher salt

1 cup chocolate chips

Preheat the oven to 350°F. Line a baking sheet with parchment paper and set aside.

In a large bowl, whisk together the **coconut sugar**, **maple syrup**, **coconut oil**, **hot water**, **vanilla extract**, and **almond extract**. Add the **oats**, **coconut**, **pecans**, **flaxseed meal**, **chia seeds**, **cinnamon**, and **salt** and toss well to combine, making sure the dry ingredients are fully coated.

Add the mixture to the prepared baking sheet and press down so the granola is in an even layer, somewhat stuck together (this is what creates the clusters!). Bake for 30 minutes, or until the granola is fragrant and lightly golden, rotating the pan halfway through.

Set the baking sheet on a cooling rack and scatter the **chocolate chips** over the warm granola. Let the granola cool completely, undisturbed—don't mix or break it up yet! The residual heat will help the chocolate chips stick to the granola

Break the cooled granola into clusters and store in an airtight container at room temperature for up to 5 days, up to 2 weeks in the refrigerator, or up to 1 month in the freezer (if you haven't experienced chilled, crispy granola, you have to try it!).

PUT A SPIN ON IT

Love everything but the chocolate? Substitute dried blueberries, dark or golden raisins, or freeze-dried strawberries.

Any Time, Any Way Banana Bread

MAKES 1 (9-INCH) LOAF

Gluten free
Dairy free

This is one of the first types of recipes that took off on the internet for me. So many people have told me, "I found you because of banana bread!" And even though I've shared a lot of variations over the years, this is the one I keep coming back to. And you'll only find this version in *this* book! Now, our family is not immune to the weird banana-overbuying vortex; I feel like kids everywhere are so hot and cold with bananas that the moment you buy some, they decide they don't like them! So I always have bananas that are ready to use in baking, and I love having this bread on hand for breakfast, lunch boxes, or snacks. You can even dress it up with sprinkles and call it birthday banana bread! And yes, this recipe will make muffins; just bake for 10 to 15 minutes in a muffin tin. (You can even freeze, then thaw in the fridge!)

- Nonstick cooking spray
- 3 medium, very ripe bananas
- 2 large eggs
- ⅓ cup maple syrup or honey
- ¼ cup avocado oil, melted coconut oil, or melted unsalted butter (avocado oil will be the most neutral, flavor-wise)
- 1 teaspoon vanilla extract
- 1¼ cups almond flour
- 1¼ cups oat flour
- 1 teaspoon baking soda
- ½ teaspoon baking powder
- ½ teaspoon kosher salt
- ½ cup semisweet chocolate chips, chopped walnuts, or frozen blueberries (truly, the world is your oyster), plus more for topping (optional)

Preheat the oven to 350°F. Spray a 9-inch loaf pan with **nonstick spray** and set aside.

In a large bowl, add the **bananas** and mash well with a fork. Add the **eggs**, **maple syrup**, **avocado oil**, and **vanilla** and whisk until smooth. Add the **almond flour**, **oat flour**, **baking soda**, **baking powder**, and **salt** and whisk again until smooth. With a silicone spatula, fold in the **chocolate chips** (if using).

Pour the batter into the prepared loaf pan and top with more chocolate chips (if using.) Bake until a cake tester or toothpick comes out clean, about 1 hour. Cover the bread with foil if you feel like the top is browning too fast.

Let the bread cool in the pan for at least 30 minutes. Transfer to a wire rack to finish cooling completely before serving.

Sneaky Green Smoothie Pancakes

FREEZER-FRIENDLY

MAKES ABOUT 12 PANCAKES

Gluten-free friendly
Nut free

These pancakes have such a special place in my heart! I first made them when my oldest was just about a year old, and I was looking for an easy finger food without much sugar. Banana is the perfect sweetener here, but you can also add a touch of syrup if you want. Basically, these are anything you'd put into a green smoothie, just in pancake form. Sometimes, I'll add blueberries, cacao nibs, or chocolate chips, but plenty of times I'll just make them plain. Make a double batch of these and keep them in the fridge or freezer for easy breakfasts or an on-the-go snack!

- 2 cups old-fashioned or quick oats
- 2 large, very ripe bananas
- 4 large eggs
- ⅔ cup packed baby spinach
- ½ cup plain Greek yogurt
- 2 teaspoons baking powder
- 1 teaspoon ground cinnamon
- Maple syrup, to sweeten the batter (optional), and for serving
- Protein powder or hemp seeds (optional)
- ½ cup dark chocolate chips or cacao nibs (optional)
- Unsalted butter, for the pan

In a blender, add the **oats**, **bananas**, **eggs**, **spinach**, **yogurt**, **baking powder**, **cinnamon**, a splash of **maple syrup** (if desired), and **protein powder** (if using) and blend until mostly smooth—we like a little texture from the oats. Add the **chocolate chips** (if using) and stir gently to combine.

In a large, nonstick skillet over medium heat, melt a small amount of **butter**. Use about ¼ cup of batter per pancake, working in batches to keep enough space between them. Cook until the pancakes start to bubble, about 5 minutes, and flip. Cook for another 2 minutes and transfer the cooked pancakes to a plate. Repeat with the remaining batter. Remove the pan from the heat.

Serve warm with maple syrup and any other desired toppings.

PUT A SPIN ON IT

Craving something other than pancakes? Make these into muffins, or mini muffins if you prefer! Bake at 350°F for 10 to 12 minutes, or until a toothpick comes out clean.

High-Protein Bacon, Egg White & Cheese "Muffins"

FREEZER-FRIENDLY

MAKES 12 MUFFINS

Gluten free
Nut free

Ahh, the bacon-egg-and-cheese . . . if you know, you know! My husband loves bacon, egg, and cheese anything, and will order it at any bagel place he can find it. But having to eat gluten-free means it can be hard to come by. This is a lighter version thanks to the turkey bacon, but it still has a lot of creaminess and protein from the cottage cheese. These are a dream to make ahead and store in the refrigerator or even freezer—they just need a minute or so in the microwave to reheat. You can change up the veggies with whatever you have on hand, and these are awesome for school lunches when you want to switch it up from sandwiches.

Nonstick cooking spray

1 tablespoon extra-virgin olive oil

1 medium red or orange bell pepper, chopped

6 slices turkey bacon, chopped

¼ cup chopped shallots

½ cup shredded zucchini, excess moisture squeezed out

¼ cup chopped fresh chives or scallions

1 (16-ounce) carton liquid egg whites

½ cup cottage cheese

½ teaspoon garlic powder

Kosher salt and freshly ground black pepper

¼ cup shredded cheddar or crumbled feta or goat cheese

Preheat the oven to 350°F. Spray a nonstick or silicone 12-cup muffin tin generously with cooking spray and set aside. If you're using a silicone muffin pan, set it over a baking sheet.

In a large skillet over medium heat, heat the **olive oil**. Add the **bell pepper**, **turkey bacon**, and **shallots** and cook, stirring frequently, until the peppers are tender, 5 to 6 minutes. Add the **zucchini** and **chives** and cook until the zucchini is tender, about 3 minutes. Remove the pan from the heat.

In a large bowl, whisk together the **egg whites**, **cottage cheese**, and **garlic powder**, and season generously with **salt** and **pepper**. Fold in the vegetable mixture.

Add about ⅓ cup of the egg mixture to the prepared muffin tin and sprinkle the **cheddar cheese** over the top of each egg muffin. Bake until the eggs are set, about 30 minutes. Set the tin on a cooling rack and let the muffins cool for at least 15 minutes before serving.

Store the egg muffins in an airtight container in the fridge for up to 1 week, or in the freezer for up to 2 months.

High-Protein Cinnamon Raisin Quick Bagels

MAKES 6 BAGELS

Gluten-free friendly
Nut free

FREEZER-FRIENDLY

Here it is, my perfect marriage of a high-protein, sweet (but not too sweet) breakfast! These bagels are my all-time favorite quick and easy breakfast for so many reasons: they freeze incredibly well, they feel cozy and sweet from the cinnamon-sugar topping, and they truly come together so fast. Unlike a traditional bagel that uses a yeasted dough, these are made more in the style of a "quick bread" (think banana or pumpkin bread) and use baking powder to rise. My one piece of advice is that you absolutely must TOAST THESE. The bagels are good as-is, but they're divine when toasted—and all the better to soak in whatever toppings you choose!

BAGELS

1 cup plain Greek yogurt

1 cup cottage cheese

1½ cups all-purpose flour, plus more for the counter, gluten-free if needed

¼ cup ground flaxseed

2 tablespoons coconut sugar

1 tablespoon plus 1 teaspoon baking powder

1 teaspoon ground cinnamon

⅓ cup dark raisins

1 large egg, lightly beaten

CINNAMON-SUGAR TOPPING

2 tablespoons unsalted butter, melted

1 tablespoon coconut sugar

1 teaspoon ground cinnamon

MAKE THE BAGELS: Preheat the oven to 400°F. Line a baking sheet with parchment paper and set aside.

In a large bowl, stir together the **yogurt** and **cottage cheese**. Add the **flour**, **flaxseed**, **coconut sugar**, **baking powder**, and **cinnamon** and mix well to combine. If the dough feels too thick or isn't holding together, add a tablespoon or two of **water**. Fold in the **raisins**.

Turn out the dough onto a lightly floured work surface. Use your hands to knead and roll the dough into a ball, adding a small amount of flour if the dough feels too sticky. Divide the dough into 6 portions. Roll each portion into about a 6-inch log and connect the ends to form a bagel shape. Add the bagel to the prepared baking sheet and repeat with the remaining dough. (It's okay if the dough cracks a little bit as you're shaping the bagels; you can simply push the dough back together once you set it on the pan.) Set aside.

MAKE THE CINNAMON-SUGAR TOPPING: In a small bowl, stir together the melted **butter**, **coconut sugar**, and **cinnamon**.

Brush the tops of the bagels with the beaten **egg**, followed by the cinnamon-sugar topping.

Bake until the bagels are slightly golden, 22 to 25 minutes. Let cool completely before eating.

To serve, slice and toast the bagels, and top as desired.

To freeze, slice and store the bagels in an airtight container or bag for up to 2 months.

Crispy Tortilla-Crusted Absolutely Loaded Quiche

SERVES 2 TO 4

Gluten-free friendly
Nut-free friendly

This one is for the savory breakfast lovers, and it's a true fridge clean-out meal! It works with any vegetables, any cheese, any protein, you name it. I typically have olives, scallions, and spinach on hand, so I gravitate toward them, but anything works, so take what's here as a suggestion. This reminds me of an old-school taco salad (you know, with the taco shell bowl!), but it's easier to put together and keeps so well in the fridge for an easy grab-and-go breakfast. I'm more of a sweet breakfast person, but *Hot tip:* This is one of my favorite dinners. You can eat this cold or at room temp, and it's a great dish for entertaining.

1 large (11- or 12-inch) flour or almond flour tortilla

4 large eggs

1 cup packed baby spinach, chopped

6 cherry tomatoes, halved

⅓ cup chopped red bell pepper

⅓ cup crumbled feta cheese, plus more for topping

8 pitted kalamata olives, roughly chopped

2 scallions, chopped (green parts only)

Kosher salt and freshly ground black pepper

Chopped fresh chives, for serving

Preheat the oven to 400°F. Press the **tortilla** into an 8-inch square baking dish and set aside.

In a medium bowl, whisk together the **eggs**, **spinach**, **tomatoes**, **bell pepper**, **feta**, **olives**, **scallions**, and **salt** and **pepper** to taste. Top with additional feta as desired. Bake until the eggs are set and the edges of the tortilla are golden, 20 to 25 minutes.

Top with chopped **chives** and serve.

Gorgeous, Stunning, Shockingly Easy-to-Make Pancake Trifle

with Berry Sauce

SERVES 6 TO 8

Gluten-free friendly
Nut free

I'm a very big birthday person: I love birthdays, I love celebrating people. And I'm a big believer that you should be celebrated from the moment you wake up, so birthday breakfast is a big deal in my house. My kids love yogurt and berries together, and the pancakes bring the cake element. Birthdays aside, I also make this for holiday brunches! I love using the Cottage Cheese Pancakes (page 49) for this, but go with whatever's easiest; if you like a boxed mix, or even store-bought frozen pancakes. The berry sauce is the key here, and it's basically foolproof.

BERRY SAUCE

- 1 tablespoon fresh lemon juice
- 1 tablespoon arrowroot flour
- 2 cups fresh blueberries and/or raspberries
- 3 tablespoons maple syrup, plus more for serving

TRIFLE

- About 20 (5-inch) pancakes, such as My Family's Absolute Favorite Cottage Cheese Pancakes (page 49), or use your go-to mix!
- 2 cups plain or vanilla yogurt of choice
- 2 cups mixed berries, such as blueberries, raspberries, blackberries, or sliced strawberries

MAKE THE BERRY SAUCE: In a small bowl, whisk together the **lemon juice** and **arrowroot flour** and set aside.

In a small saucepan over medium heat, add the **berries**, **maple syrup**, and **3 tablespoons of water**. Bring to a simmer and cook, stirring, for 4 minutes. Add the arrowroot mixture and stir to combine. Cook, stirring occasionally, until the berries are very soft and the sauce has thickened, another 3 or 4 minutes. Remove the pan from the heat and set aside.

ASSEMBLE THE TRIFLE: In a 3-quart trifle bowl or large glass bowl, layer about half of the **pancakes**, letting them overlap slightly. Add about half of the **yogurt** in an even layer, followed by half of the **berries**. Drizzle with a few spoonfuls of the **berry sauce**. Repeat with another layer of the remaining pancakes, the remaining yogurt, and the remaining berries. Drizzle with a bit more of the berry sauce, cover, and refrigerate for 30 minutes. (You can skip the chilling step if you're short on time!)

Serve with the remaining berry sauce and more maple syrup, if desired.

PREP TIP

Want to prep this the night before? Make the sauce and pancakes and store separately so they're ready for the next day. Then, assemble the trifle about 30 minutes before serving.

Yummy Granola Cups *with Yogurt*

FREEZER-FRIENDLY

MAKES 8 TO 10 GRANOLA CUPS

Gluten-free friendly
Dairy-free friendly
Nut free

This was actually one of the first recipes that I'd ever made in our 500-square-foot apartment back in Chelsea. I admit, when I first started making recipes, everything had oats involved. But in this case, oats are the perfect backbone to these tasty little cups! Even before having kids, I've always loved little finger foods—they seem a bit more fun and visually appealing. But boy, do kids LOVE the freedom to build their own meals. They love building these cups and decorating with any fruit or sprinkles. These are amazing for a kid-friendly breakfast or even an easy lunch-box addition, but they're equally great as a snack—for kids or for you!

- Nonstick cooking spray
- 1 medium banana, mashed (about ½ cup), or ½ cup unsweetened applesauce
- ¼ cup coconut oil, softened (but not melted)
- ¼ cup maple syrup
- 1 teaspoon vanilla extract
- 1 cup oat flour
- 1 cup rolled oats
- 1 teaspoon ground cinnamon
- Pinch of kosher salt
- Milk of choice (dairy or nondairy), as needed
- Vanilla Greek yogurt, for serving
- Fresh fruit, for serving
- Unsweetened coconut flakes, for serving (optional)
- Chocolate chips, for serving (optional)

Preheat the oven to 350°F. Spray a muffin tin with **nonstick spray** and set aside.

In a large bowl, add the **banana**, **coconut oil**, **maple syrup**, and **vanilla** and use a silicone spatula to combine. Add the **oat flour**, **oats**, **cinnamon**, and **salt** and mix again to combine. At this point, the mixture should hold together when pressed, but if it's still crumbly, feel free to add a tablespoon or two of **milk** to help it stick.

Add about 2 heaping teaspoons of the mixture to each of the wells in the muffin tin. Press down with a spatula or spoon to form an even base, and gently press a thin layer of the mixture up the sides. Bake until the edges are golden brown, 12 to 15 minutes. Let the granola cups cool completely in the pan.

You can serve these right away, filling each granola cup with **yogurt** and **fruit**, plus any other desired toppings. Or you can store the unfilled granola cups in an airtight container in the fridge for up to 5 days (they lose their firmness if stored at room temp), or in the freezer for up to 1 month, and add fillings right before serving.

My Family's Absolute Favorite Cottage Cheese Pancakes

FREEZER-FRIENDLY

MAKES 12 TO 14 (4-INCH) PANCAKES

Gluten-free friendly
Nut free

When I say we make these pancakes all the time, I mean it. Weekly? Every other week? They're never not in my house because they're so simple and they always work! I love that there's a touch of maple syrup built in so you don't need to add other sugar. These are what also turned me on to cottage cheese, after I realized it added so much protein, flavor, and creaminess. Even though I first shared them back in 2022, they're still one of the most popular recipes on my website to date, so I had to include them in *More, Please!* It wouldn't be complete without them.

- 4 large eggs
- 1½ cups cottage cheese
- 3 tablespoons maple syrup, plus more for serving
- 1 teaspoon vanilla extract
- 1 cup all-purpose flour, gluten-free if needed
- ½ tablespoon baking powder
- ¼ teaspoon kosher salt
- Mix-ins like blueberries, chocolate chips, sprinkles, whatever! (optional)
- Unsalted butter or avocado oil spray, for the pan
- Maple syrup, fruit, whipped coconut cream, and/or sprinkles, for serving (optional)

In a large bowl, whisk together the **eggs**, **cottage cheese**, **maple syrup**, and **vanilla** until smooth. (You can also combine the wet ingredients in a blender to break up the cottage cheese for a smoother pancake consistency.) Add the **flour**, **baking powder**, and **salt** and whisk again to combine. Fold in any mix-ins (if using).

Heat a large skillet over medium heat. Grease with **butter** or oil and scoop about ¼ cup of the batter onto the skillet. Repeat for as many pancakes as can comfortably fit in the pan, leaving an inch or so between pancakes. Cook until the pancakes start to bubble and are no longer shiny on top, 3 to 5 minutes. (If you find the pancakes are browning too quickly, reduce the heat to medium-low or low.) Flip and cook for another minute. Transfer the cooked pancakes to a plate and cover with a kitchen towel to keep warm. Repeat with the remaining batter. Remove the pan from the heat.

Serve the pancakes with **maple syrup** and any other desired toppings.

PREP TIP

If your crew flies through these as quickly as we do, double the batch! I do this almost every time I make them; otherwise we run out way too fast.

Not-a-Sugar-Bomb Healthy Muffins

FREEZER-FRIENDLY

MAKES ABOUT 9 MUFFINS

Gluten-free friendly
Dairy-free friendly

Remember years ago when every bakery was making the most enormous muffins known to mankind, and they were basically cake but in muffin form? Yeah, these are not those. Muffins are truly one of my favorite things to eat for breakfast, and these actually wholesome muffins are what I bake for my family as a great weekday breakfast or snack. There are two (!) types of vegetables in here, plus great fiber from the raisins (and who doesn't love raisins?). What I love even more is that this is a dream recipe for the freezer. Freeze a batch, and you'll have breakfast ready to go for the busiest of weeks. Just promise me one thing: you won't judge this book by its cover. These are not cute, but they are SO good.

Nonstick cooking spray or muffin tray liners

2 medium bananas, mashed (about 1 cup)

½ cup coconut sugar

⅓ cup milk of choice (dairy or nondairy)

¼ cup creamy nut butter or tahini

1 teaspoon vanilla extract

2 cups oat flour

2 teaspoons baking powder

1 teaspoon cinnamon

½ teaspoon ground ginger

¼ teaspoon kosher salt

1 cup peeled, shredded carrots

½ cup shredded zucchini, excess moisture squeezed out

⅓ cup chopped walnuts

⅓ cup dark raisins or chocolate chips

Preheat the oven to 350°F. Grease or line 9 wells of a muffin tin and set aside.

In a large bowl, whisk together the **mashed banana**, **coconut sugar**, **milk**, **nut butter**, and **vanilla**. Add the **oat flour**, **baking powder**, **cinnamon**, **ginger**, and **salt** and use a silicone spatula to combine. Gently fold in the **carrots**, **zucchini**, **walnuts**, and **raisins**, mixing well to combine.

Generously spoon the mixture into the prepared muffin tin. These don't rise much, so if it feels like you're overfilling the muffin tin, you're not!

Bake for 18 to 20 minutes, until a toothpick or cake tester comes out clean.

Let the muffins cool briefly and serve. Store leftover muffins in an airtight container in the fridge for up to 1 week. (These also freeze really well and thaw easily in the refrigerator.)

PUT A SPIN ON IT

Want to spice things up a bit? I love serving these with a smear of peanut butter, right on top of a yogurt bowl. These are the ultimate morning-glory-vibe kind of muffin!

Mini Muffins Three Ways (Like the Ones at the Store!)

FREEZER-FRIENDLY

MAKES ABOUT 24 MINI MUFFINS

Gluten-free friendly
Dairy-free friendly
Nut free

A few years ago, I did a collab with Go Nanas (one of our grt sht portfolio brands!) to make a banana bread mix, and we ended up doing kind of a dupe of those blueberry "little bites" muffins you can find at the store. The mix sold out in three weeks, and I still get requests for it! These are my take on those mini muffins, and it's totally a base recipe that you can customize depending on what your family is into, whether it's mini chocolate chips, blueberries (or any fruit), or even sprinkles. So make these for a fraction of what you'd pay for the packaged version! *Hot tip:* These are also freezer-friendly and can thaw in the fridge.

- Nonstick cooking spray
- 1¼ cups milk of choice (dairy or nondairy)
- ½ cup coconut sugar
- ⅓ cup melted unsalted butter or liquid coconut oil
- 1 large egg
- 2 teaspoons vanilla extract
- 2 cups oat flour
- 2 teaspoons baking powder
- Pinch of kosher salt
- ½ cup frozen blueberries or mini chocolate chips, or ¼ cup rainbow sprinkles

Preheat the oven to 350°F. Spray a mini muffin tin with **nonstick spray** and set aside.

In a large bowl, whisk together the **milk**, **coconut sugar**, **butter**, **egg**, and **vanilla** until smooth. Add the **oat flour**, **baking powder**, and **salt** and whisk again to combine. Gently fold in the **blueberries**.

Add a heaping tablespoon of the batter to each well in the muffin tin. Bake until lightly golden on top and a cake tester or toothpick comes out clean, about 15 minutes.

Let cool for a few minutes in the tin before serving. Store leftover muffins in an airtight container at room temperature for up to 3 days, in the fridge for up to a week, or in the freezer for up to 6 months. These thaw really well in the fridge!

CRAVEABLE

SALADS &

BOWLS

Kinda Thai-ish Noodle Salad with Steak

SERVES 4 TO 6

Gluten free
Dairy free

I confess, I pretty much make this noodle salad as an excuse to consume my Ginger Sesame Dressing (page 231) yet again. (Kidding! Kind of . . .) This dish has the best balance of all the flavors—a little sweet, a little tangy, and super savory. Also, somehow it's won over my kids, I think because of their mango obsession? The tenderness of the steak is perfection, and while I do recommend marinating it if you can, it'll still be delicious if you don't have the extra time. (P.S. If you have been to a Hillstone restaurant, this dish may remind you of something!)

STEAK

- ¼ cup extra-virgin olive oil
- 3 tablespoons coconut aminos
- 2 tablespoons fresh lime juice
- 2 tablespoons chopped fresh cilantro leaves
- 2 garlic cloves, minced
- 1 tablespoon fresh grated ginger or 1 teaspoon ground ginger
- 1 tablespoon sesame oil
- Kosher salt and freshly ground black pepper
- 1½ pounds skirt steak, excess fat trimmed

NOODLE SALAD

- 8 ounces long rice noodles, such as rice sticks or soba
- 2 cups snow peas, cut into 1-inch pieces
- 1½ cups thinly sliced red or green cabbage
- 1 large mango, peeled and diced
- 1 medium red bell pepper, sliced
- ¼ cup chopped fresh cilantro leaves
- ¼ cup chopped fresh basil leaves
- ¼ cup chopped peanuts (optional)
- 1 cup Ginger Sesame Dressing (page 231)

MAKE THE STEAK: In a medium bowl, whisk together the **olive oil**, **coconut aminos**, **lime juice**, **cilantro**, **garlic**, **ginger**, **sesame oil**, and a generous amount of **salt** and **pepper**. Place the **steak** in a resealable plastic bag, add the marinade, and move the steak around in the bag to coat. Refrigerate for at least 1 hour and up to 12 hours.

Heat a large, cast-iron skillet over medium-high heat. Remove the steak from the marinade, shaking off any excess, and place it in the hot pan. Cook until the steak is well seared underneath, about 4 minutes. Flip and continue cooking until the steak is done to your liking, 3 to 5 more minutes. Remove the pan from the heat. Transfer the steak to a plate and let rest for at least 5 minutes before slicing.

MAKE THE NOODLE SALAD: In a large pot of well-salted boiling water, cook the **rice noodles** according to the package instructions. When there is a minute or so left, add the **snow peas** to blanch them with the noodles. Remove the pot from the heat. Drain, rinse under cold water, and set aside.

In a large bowl, add the cold noodles, snow peas, **cabbage**, **mango**, **bell pepper**, **cilantro**, **basil**, and **peanuts** (if using). Add ½ cup of the **dressing** and toss well to coat.

Thinly slice the steak against the grain and add it to the salad. Drizzle a little more dressing on top, toss gently, and serve.

PREP TIP

This salad is amazing for what I think of as accidental meal prep, because when it's left over and cold straight from the fridge, it absolutely hits the spot. And if you want to swap out the protein, chicken, shrimp, and tofu all work great!

Evergreen Lemony Parmesan Kale Salad

SERVES 4

Gluten-free friendly
Nut free

Let's face it, kale, especially a raw kale salad, still has kind of a bad rap. But trust me when I tell you, this is THE best way to eat kale. I named this an evergreen salad because it truly never gets old, it goes with everything, and yes, there is a pun with the deep-green color of the dressed kale. I've been making this for myself for ages, but it turns out my kids love it too. You can serve it as-is, but it's really a knockout with nearly any protein in this book. My favorite? I top this with a Salmon Burger (page 83) because the buttery texture of the salmon goes so well with the punchy dressing and slightly bitter greens. As with most kale salads, this improves as it sits in the fridge, and you can swap out or add any vegetables or other cheeses you like.

½ cup extra-virgin olive oil

¾ cup DIY Toasted Cracker Breadcrumbs (page 223) or panko breadcrumbs

Kosher salt and freshly ground black pepper

2 to 3 bunches Italian kale, stemmed and roughly chopped (about 6 packed cups)

½ cup fresh lemon juice

1 cup grated Parmesan cheese, plus more for serving

3 garlic cloves, minced

1 cup lightly packed fresh parsley, cilantro, or basil leaves, or a mix, large leaves torn

1 avocado, sliced

Lemon wedges, for serving

Tortilla chips or crackers, for serving (optional)

In a medium skillet over medium heat, heat 2 tablespoons of the **oil**. Add the **breadcrumbs** and a small pinch of **salt** and toss to coat in the oil. Cook, stirring frequently, until the breadcrumbs are golden brown, about 5 minutes. Remove the pan from the heat and set aside.

In a large bowl, add the **kale** and drizzle with about 3 tablespoons of the **lemon juice**. Massage the kale with your hands until very tender—this will take a few minutes! Set aside.

In a medium bowl, add the remaining lemon juice and the remaining oil, plus the **Parmesan**, **garlic**, **salt** to taste, and lots of **pepper**, and whisk until smooth. Add the dressing to the massaged kale, plus the **herbs**, **avocado**, and about half of the toasted breadcrumbs, and toss gently to coat.

To serve, top with the remaining breadcrumbs and another generous sprinkle of Parmesan, with **lemon wedges** on the side. I also LOVE scooping this with **tortilla chips** or **crackers**.

WAYS TO SERVE

- Yogurt-Marinated Chicken Skewers *(page 92)*
- Jordan's Foolproof Spatchcock Chicken *(page 109)*
- Gourmet-Looking (and Tasting!) Salmon Burgers *(page 83)*

Crispy Chicken Caesar Salad

SERVES 4 TO 6

Gluten-free friendly
Nut free

You know I love anything that does double duty in a recipe, and here we're using the Caesar dressing both as a marinade (yes, marinade!) for the chicken and, of course, as a dressing for the salad. One of my sons loves salad (go figure!) and chicken Caesar wraps, so when I make this, he can go to town and I just put the chicken in a tortilla for my other two boys. You can serve this fully deconstructed to let everyone get what they want—it's super customizable! This chicken is SO good, like truly finger-licking good, guys.

CRISPY CHICKEN

1 pound boneless, skinless chicken breasts

¼ cup A Bit Lighter Greek Yogurt Caesar Dressing (page 228), or store-bought

½ teaspoon smoked paprika

Kosher salt and freshly ground black pepper

2 cups DIY Toasted Cracker Breadcrumbs (page 223) or store-bought breadcrumbs

Avocado or extra-virgin olive oil, for the pan

SALAD

6 cups chopped Romaine or butter lettuce, or shredded kale, or a mix

1½ cups A Bit Lighter Greek Yogurt Caesar Dressing (page 228), or store-bought

Grated Parmesan cheese, for serving

MAKE THE CHICKEN: Cut the **chicken breasts** into halves or thirds, horizontally, like medallions. (If the chicken breasts are thick, you can also butterfly them through the middle first.) Place the chicken between two sheets of plastic wrap or parchment paper and use a meat mallet or rolling pin to pound the chicken to ¼-inch thickness.

In a large bowl, add the chicken, **dressing**, and **smoked paprika**, and season generously with **salt** and **pepper**. Let sit for at least 15 minutes and up to 2 hours to marinate (cover and chill if you're marinating for more than an hour).

Add the **breadcrumbs** to a wide, shallow bowl or plate and set next to the stove. Set a wire rack over a baking sheet, or line a large plate with paper towels, and set on the other side of the stove.

In a large skillet over medium heat, heat about ¼ inch of **oil**. Place a piece of marinated chicken in the breadcrumbs, pressing gently to help the crumbs adhere. Add the coated chicken to the hot oil and repeat, working in batches to avoid crowding the pan. Cook the chicken until golden underneath, about 3 minutes. Turn and cook until the chicken is deep golden brown and measures 165°F on a thermometer, another 3 minutes. Transfer the cooked chicken to the wire rack and repeat with the remaining chicken. Remove the pan from the heat.

ASSEMBLE THE SALAD: In a large bowl, add the **lettuce**, about half of the **dressing**, and a handful of **Parmesan** and toss well to coat. Slice the chicken and place it on top of the salad. Serve with the remaining dressing and extra Parmesan on the side.

Chop-Chop Greek Salad
with Za'atar Chicken

SERVES 4 TO 6

Gluten free
Nut free

Unsurprisingly, given my love for Greek food, this was one of the first recipes I decided needed to go in this book! I'm a sucker for a chopped salad, and the flavors here are so punchy with the scallions, feta, and lemony dressing. And the za'atar chicken is so beautiful, incredibly juicy, and flavorful, you could really make it on its own (I do, all the time), but the chicken and the salad together are such a power couple. You can make all the components separately for a serious meal-prep dream, but it's impressive enough to make for a gathering. Also, if you don't love, say, red onions or tomatoes, omit and add something else if you'd like!

ZA'ATAR CHICKEN

⅔ cup extra-virgin olive oil

Juice of 2 lemons

½ cup chopped fresh parsley leaves, plus more for serving

8 garlic cloves, peeled and crushed

2 tablespoons za'atar seasoning, plus more for sprinkling

1 teaspoon ground paprika

½ teaspoon ground cinnamon

Kosher salt and freshly ground black pepper

1 medium red onion, thinly sliced

½ lemon, thinly sliced

4 boneless, skinless chicken breasts

DRESSING

¼ cup plus 2 tablespoons extra-virgin olive oil

2 tablespoons red wine vinegar

2 garlic cloves, minced

1 teaspoon dried oregano

Kosher salt and freshly ground black pepper

CHOPPED GREEK SALAD

1 head romaine lettuce, finely shredded

10 scallions, thinly sliced (white and green parts)

1 pint cherry tomatoes, halved

1 cup crumbled feta cheese

½ cup pitted kalamata olives

¼ medium red onion, thinly sliced

2 Persian or baby cucumbers, diced

¼ cup finely chopped fresh mint, plus more for serving

¼ cup finely chopped fresh dill, plus more for serving

Fluffy Quinoa (page 210), for serving (optional)

MAKE THE CHICKEN: In a 9x13-inch baking dish, add the **oil**, **lemon juice**, **parsley**, **garlic**, **za'atar**, **paprika**, **cinnamon**, and a generous amount of **salt** and **pepper** and whisk to combine. Add the sliced **onions** and **lemons** and toss to coat. Lay the **chicken breasts** in the marinade and turn several times to coat well, pulling some of the onion and lemon slices on top of the chicken. Cover the dish and refrigerate for at least 2 hours, and up to overnight.

Preheat the oven to 400°F.

Sprinkle more za'atar over the chicken and roast until golden and the internal temperature measures 165°F, 30 to 35 minutes. Set the chicken aside to rest.

MAKE THE DRESSING: In a medium bowl, whisk together the **oil**, **vinegar**, **garlic**, **oregano**, and **salt** and **pepper** to taste. Taste and adjust seasonings as desired and set aside.

ASSEMBLE THE SALAD: In a large bowl, add the **romaine**, **scallions**, **tomatoes**, **feta**, **olives**, **red onion**, **cucumbers**, **mint**, and **dill**. Drizzle on some of the dressing and toss well to coat.

Top the salad with the za'atar chicken, plus more dressing, parsley, dill, and mint, and serve. For a protein boost, serve the salad over or alongside a few scoops of quinoa.

At-Home Chipotle-Style Chicken Burrito Bowls

with Super-Quick Guacamole

SERVES 4 TO 6

Gluten free
Nut free

Every time my husband and I pass a Chipotle, we look at each other and one of us whispers, "Should we get it today?" And honestly, it really comes down to their chicken—it's so good and we're both obsessed. Since Jordan is The Chicken Guy in our house, he helped me crack the code on the seasoning for the chicken here. These bowls are a lot more cost-effective and the portions are much easier to manage than a huge takeout bowl. And the leftovers are great for building your own burrito, quesadilla, whatever!

CHIPOTLE CHICKEN

- 2 tablespoons extra-virgin olive oil
- 1 chipotle pepper in adobo sauce, minced (or more if you like spicy!)
- 1 teaspoon garlic powder
- 1 teaspoon ground cumin
- ½ teaspoon dried oregano
- Kosher salt and freshly ground black pepper
- 2 boneless, skinless chicken breasts or 4 boneless, skinless chicken thighs

FAJITA VEGGIES

- 1 tablespoon extra-virgin olive oil
- 2 medium red bell peppers, sliced
- 1 small white onion, sliced
- Kosher salt

SUPER-QUICK GUACAMOLE

- 1 ripe avocado
- 1 small jalapeño, seeded (if desired) and minced (optional)
- 2 tablespoons finely chopped fresh cilantro leaves
- Juice of ½ lime
- Kosher salt

FOR SERVING

- Cilantro-Lime Rice (page 214)
- Warmed black beans
- Charred corn (I like to use frozen by thawing it and warming it up)
- Mild chunky salsa
- Shredded cheddar or Jack cheese
- Plain Greek yogurt (we love to use this just like sour cream)
- Shredded lettuce
- Tortilla chips

MAKE THE CHICKEN: In a medium bowl, whisk together 1 tablespoon of the **oil**, plus the **chipotle**, **garlic powder**, **cumin**, **oregano**, and **salt** and **pepper** to taste. Place the **chicken** in a large resealable plastic bag and add the marinade. Seal the bag and work the marinade around the chicken, coating it thoroughly. Refrigerate the chicken in the marinade for at least 30 minutes and up to overnight.

In a large skillet over medium-high heat, heat the remaining tablespoon of oil. Remove the chicken from the marinade, shaking off any excess, and add it to the hot pan. Cook until the chicken reaches an internal temperature of 165°F and is deeply golden brown on each side, 5 to 7 minutes per side, depending on the thickness of your chicken. Remove the pan from the heat. Let the chicken rest for about 10 minutes, slice into strips, and set aside.

MAKE THE FAJITA VEGGIES: In a large skillet over medium-high heat, heat the **oil**. Add the **bell peppers**, **onion**, and **salt** to taste and cook, stirring frequently, until the vegetables are softened and a bit charred on the outside, 8 to 10 minutes. Remove the pan from the heat and set aside.

MAKE THE GUACAMOLE: In a medium bowl, mash together the **avocado**, **jalapeño** (if using), **cilantro**, **lime juice**, and **salt** to taste. Set aside.

SERVE: Assemble bowls as desired.

The Most Underrated Nourishing Lentil Rice Bowls

SERVES 6

Gluten free
Nut free

Is this the most random recipe in the book? Maybe! But lentils always remind me of my mother-in-law and the time we spent living with my in-laws. She's super creative and manages to throw together some of the most unexpected things, but they're still warm and nourishing and healthy. This dish is loaded with vegetables but doesn't really feel like a forkful of vegetables, you know? And the raisins add such a welcome bit of sweetness. This has plenty of protein thanks to the lentils and broth, though you can always add a dollop of yogurt or some chicken on the side.

- 2 tablespoons extra-virgin olive oil, plus more for serving
- 1 medium yellow onion, chopped
- 1 small zucchini, diced
- ½ cup peeled, diced carrots
- ⅓ cup diced celery
- 1 garlic clove, minced
- 1 teaspoon ground cumin
- ½ teaspoon ground cinnamon
- ½ teaspoon kosher salt
- 4 cups chicken stock or bone broth
- 1 cup white basmati or jasmine rice
- 1 cup French green lentils
- 1 cup dark raisins
- 2 cups finely chopped kale or baby spinach
- 1 cup crumbled feta or goat cheese, plus more for serving
- ¼ cup chopped fresh herbs of choice (optional)
- Squeeze of lemon, for serving (optional)
- Plain Greek yogurt, for serving (optional)

In a large, high-sided skillet over medium heat, heat the **oil**. Add the **onion** and cook, stirring, until translucent, about 5 minutes. Add the **zucchini**, **carrots**, and **celery** and cook, stirring frequently, until softened, 5 to 7 minutes. Stir in the **garlic**, **cumin**, **cinnamon**, and **salt** and cook until just fragrant, 1 minute. Add the **stock**, **rice**, and **lentils** and stir to combine. Increase the heat to medium-high and bring the mixture to a boil. Reduce the heat to medium-low, cover, and simmer until the stock is absorbed, about 40 minutes. Remove the pan from the heat.

Fold in the **raisins** and **kale**, cover, and let the kale wilt in the residual heat, 5 to 10 minutes. Taste and adjust the seasonings as needed. Add the **feta** and **herbs** (if using) and toss to combine.

Serve warm with additional cheese, a squeeze of **lemon**, a drizzle of olive oil, and a dollop of **yogurt** (if desired).

Protein-Boosted Veggie Quinoa Fried Rice

SERVES 4 TO 6

Gluten free
Dairy free
Nut-free friendly

We buy the ginormous bag of quinoa at Costco and I love prepping it for the week, hence why I had to put my back-pocket Fluffy Quinoa (page 210) recipe in the book. I'll usually make a big batch just to have on hand for an easy side or salad mix-in, and when I inevitably end up with extra, I always turn to this protein-packed version of fried rice. This has been among my kids' top favorite dinners for ages, and I also love putting some in their lunch boxes. There's so much protein here from the quinoa, edamame, and eggs, but you can always add chicken, tofu, leftover steak, or shrimp if you like.

- 1 tablespoon avocado oil, plus more as needed
- ½ cup chopped white onion
- 2 garlic cloves, minced
- 1½ cups frozen shelled edamame
- 1 cup peeled, shredded carrots
- 3 cups Fluffy Quinoa with a Protein Boost (page 210) or any cooked quinoa
- 1½ cups chopped or shredded cooked chicken, such as Jordan's Foolproof Spatchcock Chicken (page 109) or rotisserie chicken (optional)
- 3 large eggs, lightly beaten
- ¼ cup coconut aminos or teriyaki sauce, plus more as needed
- 3 scallions, thinly sliced (white and green parts), plus more for serving
- 2 teaspoons sesame oil
- Kosher salt
- Chopped cashews or peanuts, for serving (optional)

In a large nonstick skillet over medium-high heat, heat the **avocado oil**. Add the **onion** and **garlic** and cook, stirring, until fragrant, about 2 minutes. Add the **edamame** and **carrots** and cook, stirring frequently, until the carrots are tender, 4 to 6 minutes. Add the **quinoa**, breaking it up as you stir, plus the **chicken** (if using), and cook until warmed through, about 5 minutes. If the pan looks dry during this time, add a bit more avocado oil as needed.

Push the quinoa mixture to the sides of the pan and add the beaten **eggs**. Cook, stirring frequently, until the eggs are fully cooked, about 3 minutes. Stir in the **coconut aminos**, **scallions**, and **sesame oil** and cook until the flavors are just combined, 1 to 2 minutes. Check for seasoning, adding more coconut aminos or salt as desired. Remove the pan from the heat.

Serve warm, topped with additional scallions, sesame oil, and chopped **cashews** (if using).

Our Breakfast-for-Dinner Burrito Bowls

SERVES 4

Gluten free
Dairy-free friendly
Nut free

Fun fact about me: I don't love to eat eggs for breakfast. I love sweet things in the morning and I feel like I want savory stuff like this later on in the day, so these bowls are great for truly any meal! They have all the elements of a breakfast burrito, just in a bowl format. This is a dish I love to prep ahead of time to have up my sleeve for an easy dinner, casual company, or just to meal prep for myself.

BOWLS

3 tablespoons avocado oil

1 (15-ounce) can black beans, rinsed and drained

1 tablespoon taco seasoning

Kosher salt and freshly ground black pepper

6 Yukon Gold potatoes, cut into ½-inch cubes

1 medium orange bell pepper, diced

8 slices turkey bacon, chopped

2 tablespoons chopped scallions (green parts only)

8 large eggs

¼ cup milk of choice (dairy or nondairy)

FOR SERVING

Sliced avocado

Pico de gallo or salsa

Shredded cheddar cheese

Plain Greek yogurt or sour cream

Chopped fresh cilantro leaves

Lime wedges

MAKE THE BOWLS: In a small saucepan over medium heat, heat 1 tablespoon of the **oil**. Add the **beans** and ½ tablespoon of the **taco seasoning** and cook, stirring occasionally, until the beans are warmed through. Remove the pan from the heat and add **salt** and **pepper** to taste. Set aside.

In a large, nonstick skillet over medium-high heat, heat another tablespoon of the oil. Add the **potatoes**, **bell pepper**, and the remaining ½ tablespoon of taco seasoning. Cook, stirring frequently, until the pepper is softened and the potatoes begin to brown, about 10 minutes. Add the **turkey bacon** and **scallions** and reduce the heat to medium. Continue cooking, stirring occasionally, until the potatoes are tender, another 10 to 12 minutes. Remove the pan from the heat. Divide the mixture among bowls and set aside.

In a medium bowl, crack the **eggs** and add the **milk**. Whisk until smooth.

Return the skillet to medium-high heat and add the remaining tablespoon of oil. Add the egg mixture to the skillet and cook, stirring occasionally, until the eggs are done to your liking, 5 to 8 minutes. Remove the pan from the heat.

ASSEMBLE: Top 4 bowls with the scrambled eggs and a few spoonfuls of the warm black beans. Serve with any desired toppings.

PUT A SPIN ON IT

Want to turn these into tacos or give them more of a burrito vibe? Add the fillings to your favorite tortilla, or better yet, go full nacho bowl and scoop with tortilla chips!

Crispy Rice Bowls
with Ginger Sesame Dressing

SERVES 4

Gluten free
Dairy free

Oddly enough, my husband was the first person to play around with this back when we lived in Hoboken in 2018, just looking to do something different with leftover rice. It feels like you've always got leftover rice, and instead of going straight to reheating it, it's so easy to make this grain salad. It's amazing with basically any protein from this book, but it's also just as easy to top with a fried or hard-boiled egg. It can also very much be a kitchen-sink dish for any vegetables that need using up. And this dressing? So addictive, it's in a few different places in this book! One note: Definitely check the heat level on your red curry paste before deciding how much to use. Some brands are spicier than others!

3 tablespoons extra-virgin olive oil

2 teaspoons red curry paste, plus more depending on your curry paste and heat preference

3 cups My Tried & True Rice (page 213) or any cooked jasmine or basmati rice

1 tablespoon arrowroot or tapioca flour

1 cup Ginger Sesame Dressing (page 231)

½ large English cucumber, thinly sliced

¼ cup chopped fresh cilantro leaves

½ cup roughly chopped nuts or seeds, such as peanuts, cashews, or sunflower seeds

1 medium shallot, thinly sliced

1 avocado, sliced

Any cooked protein, such as hard-boiled or fried eggs, Jordan's Foolproof Spatchcock Chicken (page 109), Juicy Caramelized Onion Turkey Burgers (page 124), or Gourmet-Looking Salmon Burgers (page 83)

Preheat the oven to 425°F. Line a baking sheet with parchment paper and set aside.

In a large bowl, whisk together the **oil** and **curry paste**. Add the **rice** and toss well to coat. Add the **arrowroot flour** and toss again to coat. The mixture should start to stick together a bit, but if it looks dry, you can add a splash of water. Use your hands to gently squeeze large chunks of rice together and transfer them to the prepared baking sheet.

Bake until crispy and fragrant, 8 to 10 minutes. Break the rice into smaller, bite-sized chunks. From here, you can return the rice to the oven to crisp up a little more.

Add the crispy rice to a large bowl and toss with about half of the **dressing**. Add the **cucumber**, **cilantro**, **nuts**, and **shallot** and toss again. Top the salad with **avocado** and your desired **protein**, plus an extra drizzle of dressing, and serve.

SAFE SWAP

Got leftover quinoa in the fridge? Use that instead! It's another great option.

Fully Loaded BLT Salad

with a Quick Ranch Dressing

SERVES 2 TO 4

Gluten free
Nut free

This is a salad I'm always craving, even if I'm not necessarily in a salad mood. Does that even make sense? Hear me out: For me it's the creamy, chive-y ranch dressing, plus the classic BLT combo taken to a whole new level with avocado, corn, and feta cheese. See? You're salivating too. And the combination of bitter arugula and sweet butter lettuce is my favorite greens base. You can totally shortcut this and use rotisserie chicken, or use Jordan's Foolproof Spatchcock Chicken recipe (page 109). This is amazing to prep for weekday lunches at home, easy summer dinners, or even to bring to a barbecue.

3 cups roughly chopped butter lettuce

3 cups roughly chopped baby arugula

2 cups chopped, cooked chicken, such as Jordan's Foolproof Spatchcock Chicken (page 109) or store-bought rotisserie chicken

2 cups (1 pint) grape tomatoes, quartered

1 cup fresh or frozen and thawed sweet corn

½ cup Too-Easy-Not-to-Make Ranch Dressing (page 228), plus more as needed

1 cup (6 ounces) crumbled feta or goat cheese

1 medium avocado, cubed

6 slices thick-cut bacon, cooked and chopped

Kosher salt and freshly ground black pepper

In a large bowl, add the **lettuce**, **arugula**, **chicken**, **tomatoes**, and **corn**. Add the **dressing** and toss well to coat. Gently fold in the **feta**, **avocado**, and **bacon**. Season to taste with **salt** and **pepper** and add more dressing as desired.

Serve immediately. If prepping ahead of time, add the avocado and dressing just before serving.

SAFE SWAP

Both turkey and pork bacon will work here, so use what you love! Turkey bacon is my fave and I love it in this salad.

YES, YOU CAN COOK FIS

H

20-Minute Quicker-than-Takeout Shrimp Teriyaki

SERVES 4 TO 6

Gluten free
Dairy free
Nut free

Growing up, when we did get takeout, it was always either pizza or Chinese food. And I still do love some occasional takeout! Because seriously, sometimes you're not in the mood, it's been a long day, and you simply can't handle the thought of washing a single pan. But if you've got even an ounce of energy, I'm here to tell you this is faster than almost any takeout turnaround time, and the veggies here are so crisp and fresh—something that doesn't always happen by the time the takeout gets to your house.

TERIYAKI SAUCE

- 1 tablespoon arrowroot or tapioca flour
- 2 tablespoons cold water
- ¼ cup coconut aminos
- 2 tablespoons coconut sugar
- 1 tablespoon honey
- 2 teaspoons minced garlic
- 2 teaspoons fresh grated ginger, or 1 teaspoon ground ginger
- 1 teaspoon sesame oil

STIR-FRY

- 2 tablespoons avocado oil
- 3 cups snow peas
- 2 medium red or orange bell peppers, sliced
- Kosher salt and freshly ground black pepper
- 1¼ pounds uncooked, peeled, and deveined large shrimp, fresh or frozen and thawed, patted dry
- My Tried & True Rice (page 213) or Fluffy Quinoa (page 210), for serving
- Sliced scallions, for serving
- Sesame seeds, for serving

MAKE THE SAUCE: In a small bowl, whisk the **arrowroot flour** with the **cold water** and set aside.

In a small saucepan over medium-high heat, add the **coconut aminos**, **coconut sugar**, **honey**, **garlic**, **ginger**, and **sesame oil**, plus **½ cup of water**. Cook, stirring, until the coconut sugar is dissolved, about 3 minutes. Increase the heat to high and bring the sauce to a boil. Add the arrowroot mixture and cook, stirring, until the sauce has thickened, about 2 more minutes. Remove the pan from the heat and set aside.

MAKE THE STIR-FRY: In a large skillet over medium-high heat, heat 1 tablespoon of the **avocado oil**. Add the **snow peas**, **bell peppers**, and **salt** and **pepper** to taste and cook, stirring frequently, until the vegetables have started to brown and soften but are still crisp, 3 to 5 minutes. Remove the pan from the heat and transfer the vegetables to a plate.

Return the pan to medium-high heat and add the remaining tablespoon of oil. Add the **shrimp**, plus salt and pepper to taste, and cook, stirring frequently, until the shrimp is pink and just cooked through, 2 to 3 minutes. Return the vegetables to the pan and add the sauce. Toss well to combine and cook until warmed through, 1 to 2 minutes. Remove the pan from the heat.

Serve over the **rice** or **quinoa** and top with sliced **scallions** and **sesame seeds**.

SAFE SWAP

If you're not into shrimp, you can sub out chicken or tofu! It's honestly all about the sauce here.

Crispy Baked Sheet Pan Fish & "Chips"

SERVES 4 TO 6

Gluten free
Dairy free

This recipe is all about Glenn, my father-in-law. Every time we go out for dinner with my husband's family, Glenn is always on the hunt for fish & chips on the menu. It's his favorite! (He's also the resident fish guy in the family—he grills *the best* salmon.) This is definitely more of an homage to the classic dish: it's healthier, we're not deep-frying anything, but it still hits those spots of cozy comfort. It's a great option if you love fish & chips but want to avoid the mess (and smell, let's be real) of fried fish at home. The tartar sauce really ties it together, but you can also serve this with ketchup or any other favorite condiments.

CHIPS

2 medium russet potatoes, cut into thin wedges

1 tablespoon avocado oil

1 teaspoon kosher salt

1 teaspoon freshly ground black pepper

FISH

1 large egg

½ cup almond flour

¼ cup tapioca or arrowroot flour

1 teaspoon garlic powder

1 teaspoon onion powder

1 teaspoon ground paprika

½ teaspoon kosher salt

4 small cod fillets (about 1½ pounds), or halibut

Flaky salt, for sprinkling (optional)

Lemon wedges, for serving

TARTAR SAUCE

½ cup mayonnaise

2 teaspoons diced dill pickle or pickle relish

½ teaspoon Dijon or yellow mustard

½ teaspoon dried dill, or 1 teaspoon chopped fresh dill

½ teaspoon fresh lemon juice, plus more as needed

MAKE THE CHIPS: Preheat the oven to 400°F. Line two baking sheets with parchment paper. Set a wire rack on one of the baking sheets and set both aside.

In a large bowl, add the **potato wedges**, **avocado oil**, **salt**, and **pepper** and toss well to coat. Lay the potatoes on the prepared baking sheet (without the rack) in an even layer. Bake until very tender inside and crispy along the edges, about 30 minutes.

MAKE THE FISH: In a wide, shallow bowl, lightly beat the **egg**. In another wide, shallow bowl, whisk together the **almond flour**, **tapioca flour**, **garlic powder**, **onion powder**, **paprika**, and **salt**.

Pat the **fish fillets** very dry with a paper towel. Dip a piece of fish in the egg, turning it to coat. Add it to the flour mixture and gently press the mixture onto the fish on all sides to coat well. Place the dredged fish on the wire rack and repeat with the remaining fillets.

Bake the fish until golden and crisp, and flakes well when pierced with a fork, 15 to 20 minutes. Sprinkle with **flaky salt** (if using) and set aside to cool slightly.

MAKE THE TARTAR SAUCE: In a medium bowl, add the **mayonnaise**, **pickle**, **mustard**, **dill**, and **lemon juice** and stir to combine. Add more lemon juice if desired.

Serve the fish and chips with **lemon wedges** and the tartar sauce on the side.

WAYS TO SERVE

- Better than Fresh, Frozen Broccoli in the Oven *(page 221)*
- Caesar Salad *(page 60)*
- Evergreen Lemony Parmesan Kale Salad *(page 59)*

One-Skillet Lemony Shrimp & Asparagus Orzo

SERVES 4 TO 6

Gluten-free friendly
Nut free
Dairy-free friendly

This one goes out to my friend who called me out on my lack of shrimp recipes! She's also a mom of three and is always looking for something that's easy but satisfying. This is something you can make with little ones around that *feels* gourmet, but really is a simple, one-skillet kind of meal. It's light and fresh, and somehow the asparagus and shrimp make it feel a bit elegant. I know shrimp can be a little intimidating, but it's so simple here and it cooks so quickly. Not all of my kids have come around to shrimp yet, but they adore orzo, and the pasta can be cooked in bone broth, so I don't worry about them skipping the main protein and just focusing on the other parts of the dish. Plus, I'm all about exposure: just because they don't like something the first couple of times doesn't mean they never will.

1 pound uncooked, peeled, and deveined shrimp, fresh or frozen and thawed

Kosher salt and freshly ground black pepper

¼ cup extra-virgin olive oil

2 large shallots, minced

1¼ cups orzo pasta

4 garlic cloves, minced

2½ cups chicken stock or bone broth, plus more as needed

½ pound fresh asparagus, trimmed and cut into 2-inch pieces

2 tablespoons finely chopped fresh parsley leaves, plus more for serving

Grated zest and juice of 1 lemon, plus lemon wedges for serving

Grated Parmesan cheese, for serving (optional)

Thoroughly pat the **shrimp** dry with a paper towel and season generously with **salt** and **pepper**.

In a large skillet over medium-high heat, heat 2 tablespoons of the **oil**. Add the shrimp in an even layer and cook, undisturbed, until the underside is just pink, about 3 minutes. Flip and cook for another minute. Remove the pan from the heat and transfer the shrimp to a plate.

Return the pan to medium-high heat and add the remaining 2 tablespoons of oil. Add the **shallots** and cook, stirring frequently, until just translucent, about 2 minutes. Add the **orzo** and **garlic** and cook, stirring, until the orzo is lightly toasted and the garlic is fragrant, about 1 minute. Add the **stock** and season well with salt and pepper. Bring the mixture to a boil, reduce the heat to medium-low, and cover. Simmer, stirring occasionally, until the orzo is nearly cooked but still has some bite, about 10 minutes. If the pan looks dry during this time, feel free to add more stock as needed. Stir in the **asparagus** and shrimp, cover again, and continue cooking until the asparagus is just tender, 3 to 5 minutes. Remove the pan from the heat and stir in the **parsley**, **lemon zest**, and **lemon juice**.

Serve hot, topped with more parsley, a squeeze of **lemon**, and **Parmesan** (if using).

Gourmet-Looking *(and Tasting!)* Salmon Burgers *with Herby Tzatziki*

SERVES 6

Gluten free

Growing up, we used to get these salmon burgers from Costco that I loved. As I got older, my love of salmon burgers didn't change, but I started paying more attention to ingredients and realized I wanted to make salmon burgers of my own. We all know that salmon is a fish we should be eating more of, and this is a really fun way to make it instead of just shoving a few fillets in the oven. And because I am an absolute sucker for all things Greek food, I've always loved pairing these burgers with the creamy herbiness of tzatziki—it's such a fresh combination!

- 1½ pounds fresh salmon, skin and any pin-bones removed, cut into large cubes
- 2 scallions, thinly sliced (green parts only)
- Juice of ½ lemon
- 2 tablespoons finely chopped fresh chives
- 2 tablespoons finely chopped fresh parsley leaves
- 1 tablespoon whole-grain mustard
- ½ teaspoon kosher salt
- ½ teaspoon freshly ground black pepper
- Pinch of ground cayenne pepper (optional)
- ⅓ cup almond flour
- Avocado oil, for the pan
- Yogurt Tzatziki Sauce (page 116), for serving
- Hamburger buns, English muffins, or lettuce wraps, for serving (or toss the burgers on top of any of the craveable bowls in this book!)
- Pickled Red Onions and Cucumbers (page 116), for serving

In a food processor, add about three-quarters of the **salmon** and pulse until the salmon becomes a rough paste. Transfer the salmon to a large bowl and set aside.

Cut the remaining salmon into a small dice and add it to the bowl. Add the **scallions**, **lemon juice**, **chives**, **parsley**, **mustard**, **salt**, **pepper**, and **cayenne** (if using). Use a silicone spatula to gently mix until combined.

Add the **almond flour** to a wide, shallow bowl. Using your hands (use food-handling gloves here), divide the salmon mixture into 6 portions. Form a portion into a patty shape, lay it in the almond flour, and press gently to help the flour adhere, forming a crust. Set the patty aside on a plate and repeat with the remaining salmon mixture and almond flour. If it feels like the mixture is a little slippery here, don't worry! It will hold together well once it's cooked.

In a large skillet over medium heat, heat a thin layer of **avocado oil**. Add a few of the salmon patties, however many will fit without overcrowding, and cook until well browned underneath, about 4 minutes. Flip and cook until the burgers are nicely browned and the internal temperature reaches 145°F, another 4 minutes or so. Transfer the cooked burgers to a clean plate and repeat with the remaining patties. Remove the pan from the heat.

Top the burgers with a generous dollop of **tzatziki** and **pickled red onions** and **cucumbers**, then serve on your bun or wrap of choice.

WAYS TO SERVE

- No-Fryer-Added French Fries *(page 218)*
- Crispy Rice Bowls *(page 71)*
- Chop-Chop Greek Salad *(page 63)*

Shrimp & Corn Cakes
with Avocado Salsa

SERVES 4

Gluten free
Dairy free
Nut free

For this book, I wanted to play around with recipes that were nostalgic to me. When I was growing up, my mom cooked dinner at home at least five nights a week, and growing up in New Jersey meant we ate *a lot* of crab cakes. For as fancy as they might appear, they're actually pretty easy to make. I've swapped the crab for shrimp, which is a little more cost-effective and easier to find, and created a take on a crab cake I'd feed my family. These could be a great lighter bite before a meal (you could even make them mini!), or are just a great light lunch or dinner.

AVOCADO SALSA

- 3 Roma tomatoes, seeded and diced
- 2 avocados, diced
- ½ small red onion, chopped
- ¼ cup chopped fresh parsley leaves
- 1 small shallot, minced
- 1 jalapeño, seeded and minced (optional)
- Juice of 1 lime
- ¼ teaspoon salt
- ¼ teaspoon garlic powder

SHRIMP AND CORN CAKES

- 12 ounces peeled, deveined fresh shrimp, tails removed, shrimp patted dry
- 1 cup frozen sweet corn, thawed
- ⅓ cup lightly packed fresh parsley leaves
- 1 large egg
- 1½ teaspoons Old Bay Seasoning
- Kosher salt and freshly ground black pepper
- 2 tablespoons extra-virgin olive oil, plus more as needed

MAKE THE AVOCADO SALSA: In a medium bowl, add the **tomatoes**, **avocados**, **onion**, **parsley**, **shallot**, **jalapeño** (if using), **lime juice**, **salt**, and **garlic powder** and toss to combine. Cover and refrigerate while you make the shrimp cakes.

MAKE THE SHRIMP AND CORN CAKES: In a food processor, add the **shrimp** and pulse just until roughly chopped. Add the **corn**, **parsley**, **egg**, **Old Bay**, and **salt** and **pepper** to taste and pulse again, just until the mixture is finely chopped. Transfer the mixture to a medium bowl and set aside.

In a large skillet over medium-high heat, heat the **oil**. Add a very small amount of the shrimp mixture to test your seasoning. Cook for 1 or 2 minutes, until golden. Taste and adjust the seasoning as needed.

Use ¼ cup measure to scoop the shrimp mixture into the hot pan. Use the back of the measuring cup, or a spoon, to flatten the mixture into a ¼-inch-thick cake. Repeat with a few more shrimp cakes, as many as can comfortably fit in the skillet. Cook until golden and crisp on both sides, about 3 minutes per side. Transfer to a serving plate and repeat with the remaining shrimp mixture, adding more oil to the pan as needed. Remove the pan from the heat.

Top the shrimp cakes with the chilled avocado salsa and serve.

PUT A SPIN ON IT

Add more jalapeño if you want things *realllll* spicy, or omit it altogether if you're not into the heat!

WAYS TO SERVE

- Fluffy Quinoa *(page 210)*
- Cilantro-Lime Rice *(page 214)*
- Evergreen Lemony Parmesan Kale Salad *(page 59)*

Mediterranean-Style Stuffed Salmon

SERVES 4

Gluten free
Nut free

I am so excited to finally share this dish with you guys! I make this for dinner at least three times per month, it's that good. I've always loved salmon, and you know that Greek flavors are my favorite. I also feel like stuffed salmon is so underrated! Like people make stuffed chicken breasts all the time, but this is actually a lot easier and less of a production than the fuss of butterflying a chicken breast and then fighting with a toothpick to keep it closed. Forget all that and make this instead. I adore this with Chop-Chop Greek Salad (page 63) because I am a fiend, but your sides are up to you!

4 (6-ounce) salmon portions (longer, thicker pieces of salmon work best), skin left on

Extra-virgin olive oil

Kosher salt and freshly ground black pepper

3 cups loosely packed baby spinach, chopped

½ teaspoon garlic powder

¼ teaspoon dried oregano

½ teaspoon smoked paprika

1½ cups crumbled feta cheese

¼ cup grated Parmesan cheese

¼ cup chopped jarred roasted red peppers

Preheat the oven to 400°F. Line a baking sheet with parchment paper.

Place the **salmon** on the prepared baking sheet with the skin side down. Using a sharp knife and without slicing through the skin, slice a deep, lengthwise slit down the middle of each piece of salmon, leaving about ½ inch of the fish intact on either end. Brush the salmon with **oil** and season well with **salt** and **pepper**. Set aside.

In a large skillet over medium-high heat, heat about 1 tablespoon of olive oil. Add the **spinach**, **garlic powder**, **oregano**, **smoked paprika**, and **salt** and **pepper** to taste and cook, stirring frequently, until the spinach is wilted, 3 to 4 minutes. Remove the pan from the heat and stir in the **feta**, **Parmesan**, and **roasted red peppers**. Taste and adjust seasoning as needed.

Divide the spinach-feta mixture evenly among the salmon portions, gently pressing the mixture into the slit. Bake until the salmon flakes in the thickest part and measures 145°F, 15 to 20 minutes. We tend to let ours go on the long side because we like the top a bit crispy! You can also broil the salmon for a few minutes at the end for a crisp, golden top.

Serve hot.

WAYS TO SERVE

- Chop-Chop Greek Salad *(page 63)*
- Absolutely the Best-Ever Italian Pasta Salad *(page 144)*
- Lemon-Parsley Rice *(page 214)*

Tuna Patty Melt Sammies

MAKES 8 PATTIES

Gluten free
Nut free

Okay, please tell me I'm not alone in this conundrum: You're in the kitchen, it's mealtime, you've got no proteins ready at hand (maybe nothing's defrosted or it's just the end of the week!), and you're not in the mood for pasta. This is the moment I look to a recipe like this that truly makes the best use of pantry staples. I always have a few cans of tuna knocking around in the cabinet (I stock up at Costco), and within minutes I have a protein-packed diner fave that feels nostalgic and fresh at the same time. We're doing a classic tuna melt here, but you can also serve it as a tuna cake with a veggie side or on top of a salad.

TUNA PATTIES

- 2 (5-ounce) cans wild-caught tuna in water, well drained
- ½ cup chopped fresh parsley leaves
- 2 large eggs, lightly beaten
- 2 tablespoons plain Greek yogurt or mayonnaise
- 2 tablespoons Dijon mustard
- 2 teaspoons minced garlic
- Kosher salt and freshly ground black pepper
- ¼ cup extra-virgin olive oil

MELTS

- Sliced bread or buns, toasted if desired
- Sliced tomatoes
- Sliced cheese, such as cheddar or provolone
- Sliced avocado
- Crisp lettuce leaves

MAKE THE PATTIES: In a medium bowl, add the **tuna** and use a fork to break it up into flaky pieces. Add the **parsley**, **eggs**, **yogurt**, **Dijon**, **garlic**, and **salt** and **pepper** to taste and mix gently until combined.

In a large skillet over medium heat, heat the **oil**. Scoop about ¼ cup of the tuna mixture into the skillet and flatten it with the back of a fork. Repeat with however many patties can fit in the skillet without overcrowding, working in batches as needed. Cook, undisturbed, until the underside is golden brown, 3 to 4 minutes. Flip and cook until golden, another 3 minutes or so. Transfer the cooked tuna patties to a plate and repeat with the remaining mixture. Remove the pan from the heat.

MAKE THE MELTS: Preheat the broiler. Set a wire rack over a baking sheet.

Place 8 slices of **bread** on the rack, followed by a tuna patty on each. Top with a slice of **tomato**, followed by a slice of **cheese**. Broil until the cheese is just melted and beginning to bubble, about 3 minutes, watching carefully.

Top with **avocado** and/or **lettuce** as desired and serve.

SAFE SWAP

Have canned salmon in the pantry? Easy-peasy substitute here!

WAYS TO SERVE

- Evergreen Lemony Parmesan Kale Salad *(page 59)*
- No-Fryer-Added French Fries *(page 218)*
- My Go-To Japanese Sweet Potato Wedges *(page 217)*

NOT-SO-BORING CHICKEN

Juicy Yogurt-Marinated Chicken Skewers

SERVES 4 TO 6

Gluten free
Nut free

I was on a playdate with my son recently and noticed the dad was marinating chicken in mayonnaise. It makes sense—mayo does help keep the chicken tender and moist—but yogurt has that same benefit, while offering more from a nutritional standpoint! Let the chicken marinate for at least 30 minutes (overnight is even better), and it comes out perfect, not dry. Jordan, our resident Chicken Guy, dreamed up the seasoning for this marinade, and we tend to grill these on the weekends to have for the week ahead. The chicken is great warm, straight from the grill or oven, but I also love it cold to throw on salads or grains. Plus, it is so gorgeous! The color gets me every time.

- ⅓ cup plain Greek yogurt
- ⅓ cup extra-virgin olive oil
- Juice of 1 lemon
- Juice of 1 lime
- 2 tablespoons chopped fresh parsley leaves
- 2 tablespoons Dijon mustard
- 1 teaspoon garlic powder
- 1 teaspoon onion powder
- ½ teaspoon ground turmeric
- Kosher salt and freshly ground black pepper
- 2 pounds boneless, skinless chicken breasts or thighs, cut into 1-inch cubes
- Delectable Chimichurri Sauce (page 227), for serving (optional)
- Creamy, Pour-It-on-Everything Feta Sauce (page 226), for serving (optional)

In a large bowl, whisk together the **yogurt**, **oil**, **lemon juice**, **lime juice**, **parsley**, **Dijon**, **garlic powder**, **onion powder**, **turmeric**, and **salt** and **pepper** to taste. Add the cubed **chicken** and toss well to coat it in the marinade. Cover the bowl and refrigerate for at least 1 hour, and up to overnight.

Preheat the oven to 400°F. Line a baking sheet with foil, set a wire rack over the baking sheet, and set aside.

Using your hands (I like to use food-handling gloves here), assemble the skewers. Thread several pieces of chicken onto a metal skewer and set the skewer on the prepared rack. The amount of chicken per skewer will vary depending on the size of your skewers. Repeat with the remaining chicken.

Roast the chicken until golden and slightly charred, and a middle piece measures an internal temperature of 165°F, anywhere from 20 to 35 minutes (again depending on the size of your skewers). If you like a little more char on your skewers, you can set them under the broiler for a few minutes at the end.

Let the chicken cool slightly and serve with **chimichurri** and **feta sauce**, if desired.

WAYS TO SERVE

- Crispy Rice Bowls *(page 71)*
- Lemon-Parsley Rice *(page 214)*
- The Most Underrated Nourishing Lentil Rice Bowls (page 67)

Chicken Noodle Soup

(with a Twist)

FREEZER-FRIENDLY

MAKES ABOUT 2 QUARTS

Gluten free
Dairy free
Nut free

What is it about chicken soup that has always sounded so intimidating to me? You too? This is my husband's nana's chicken soup recipe and my kids love it so much, they drink the broth out of a cup. And it turns out that it's so quick to make! This is the kind of recipe that one might say "stays in the family," but you guys are my family and you also need in on this. The parsnips and turnips might seem random, but believe it or not, they add so much depth and flavor. This is one of those recipes that I make on a cozy Sunday at home and immediately stash half in the freezer for another time.

2 tablespoons extra-virgin olive oil

1¼ pounds boneless, skinless chicken thighs

Kosher salt and freshly ground black pepper

3 large carrots, peeled and diced

3 large celery stalks, diced

1 medium yellow onion, diced

3 garlic cloves, minced

1 teaspoon dried oregano

2 cups chicken stock or bone broth

1 small parsnip, peeled and cut into quarters

1 small turnip, peeled and cut into quarters

2 dried bay leaves

1 heaping cup short pasta, such as elbows or fusilli

2 tablespoons chopped fresh parsley leaves

Juice of 1 lemon

In a large Dutch oven or other heavy pot over medium-high heat, heat the **oil**. Add the **chicken** and season generously with **salt** and **pepper**. Sear the chicken until golden brown, 3 to 5 minutes per side. Remove the pot from the heat and transfer the chicken to a plate.

Return the pot to medium heat and add the **carrots**, **celery**, and **onion**, and season with **salt** and **pepper**. Cook, stirring occasionally, until the vegetables have softened, 5 to 7 minutes. Add the **garlic** and **oregano** and cook, stirring, until fragrant, another minute. Add **6 cups of water**, plus the **stock**, **parsnip**, **turnip**, **bay leaves**, and the chicken. Increase the heat to medium-high and bring to a boil. Reduce the heat to medium-low, cover, and simmer until the chicken is cooked through and the parsnip and turnip are very soft, about 15 minutes. Remove the pot from the heat. Transfer the chicken to a cutting board and use two forks to shred it into bite-sized pieces.

Using an immersion blender, blend the soup until smooth. Return the pot to medium heat and add the **pasta** to the soup, along with the shredded chicken. Cook, stirring occasionally, until the pasta is tender, 10 to 12 minutes. Remove the pot from the heat and stir in the **parsley** and **lemon juice**.

Divide among bowls and serve.

SAFE SWAP

Prefer white meat? You can swap in chicken breasts for the thighs. Or do half dark and half white meat (I feel like thighs add such great flavor)!

Our Staple, Dare I Say Meal-Prep-Worthy Chicken Salad

MAKES ABOUT 5 CUPS

Gluten free

A good chicken salad is one of those recipes that I feel like pretty much anyone will eat. And sure, this is why it's at just about every deli and grocery store, but a homemade version always seems to taste so much better! Even though you know I'm not strictly a meal prepper, this is absolutely a meal-prep dream. As you might imagine, this is even better the next day once the flavors have had time to mingle (it's all about that Dijon mustard, baby!). My kids love this on mini crackers, and I love to scoop it with crackers too, or serve over some sourdough or in lettuce wraps.

½ cup plain Greek yogurt, plus more as needed

¼ cup chopped fresh parsley leaves, dill, and/or chives (optional, but I am team chives!)

3 scallions, thinly sliced (white and green parts)

1 tablespoon Dijon mustard

Kosher salt and freshly ground black pepper

3 cups chopped or shredded cooked chicken, such as Jordan's Foolproof Spatchcock Chicken (page 109) or store-bought rotisserie chicken

1 cup diced celery

½ cup chopped cooked turkey bacon

½ cup toasted slivered almonds

In a large bowl, whisk together the **yogurt**, **herbs**, **scallions**, **Dijon**, and **salt** and **pepper** to taste. Add the **chicken**, **celery**, **turkey bacon**, and **almonds** and use a silicone spatula to combine. Add more yogurt if desired, plus additional salt and pepper as needed.

Store in an airtight container in the fridge for up to 1 week. Serve on your favorite bread or in wraps, use in lettuce wraps, or on a bed of arugula or other mixed greens, topped with avocado, tomato, and any other fixings you like. My personal go-to: a toasted everything bagel, a scoop of chicken salad, Pickled Red Onions (see page 116), and arugula—boom!

Crispy Chicken Burger Sammies

SERVES 6

Gluten free
Dairy-free friendly

My husband adores crispy chicken sandwiches, so I wanted to create a healthier version that's also easier to make at home. The thing about a whole chicken breast is that it can be juicy in one part but dry in another, the cooking time gets weird, and it just stresses me out. This is why I love using ground chicken for this recipe! It stays moist and flavorful, and it cooks a lot faster. I love putting mine in a lettuce wrap, but you can build any kind of burger or sandwich you like. And the special sauce comes in clutch here—it totally completes the burger vibes, and my kids always love it as a dip.

BURGERS

1½ pounds ground chicken

¾ cup almond flour

1 large egg, lightly beaten

1 teaspoon kosher salt

½ teaspoon freshly ground black pepper

½ teaspoon garlic powder

½ teaspoon smoked paprika

Avocado oil, for the pan

2 cups panko breadcrumbs or DIY Breadcrumbs (page 223)

Sliced cheddar cheese (optional)

FOR SERVING

Toasted hamburger buns or lettuce wraps

Better-than-the-Restaurant Special Sauce (page 226)

DIY Ketchup (page 225) or store-bought

Pickled Red Onions (page 116)

Sliced avocado

WAYS TO SERVE

- My Go-To Japanese Sweet Potato Wedges *(page 217)*
- Absolutely the Best-Ever Italian Pasta Salad *(page 144)*
- Better than Fresh, Frozen Broccoli in the Oven *(page 221)*

MAKE THE CHICKEN BURGERS: Line a baking sheet with parchment paper and set aside.

In a large bowl, add the **chicken**, **almond flour**, **egg**, **salt**, **pepper**, **garlic powder**, and **smoked paprika** and use a silicone spatula or your hands (I like using food-handling gloves) to combine. Divide the chicken mixture into 6 equal portions, shape each portion into a roughly ¾-inch-thick patty, and place on the prepared baking sheet. Repeat with the remaining chicken mixture and chill the patties for 30 minutes.

Preheat the oven to 300°F. Line a baking sheet with parchment paper, set a wire rack on the baking sheet, and set aside.

In a large, nonstick skillet over medium-high heat, heat ¼ cup of **avocado oil**.

Add the **breadcrumbs** to a wide, shallow bowl. Coat each chicken patty in the breadcrumbs, pressing down gently to make sure each is thoroughly coated. Add the coated chicken patty to the hot pan and cook, undisturbed, until the underside is deeply golden and crispy, about 3 minutes. Flip and cook until golden, another 3 minutes. Transfer the chicken burger to the wire rack and repeat with the remaining burgers, adding more oil to the skillet as needed. Remove the pan from the heat.

Top each chicken burger with a slice of **cheese** (if using). Bake the burgers until an internal thermometer reads 165°F, about 10 minutes.

SERVE: Assemble the burgers with any desired toppings. I really do think the **Special Sauce** is a nonnegotiable here, but you do you!

One-Pot Creamy Mushroom Chicken & Rice

SERVES 4 TO 6

Gluten-free friendly
Dairy-free friendly
Nut free

If I'm making a protein and a carb in the same meal, ten times out of ten, I'm throwing them together in a skillet. This dish really is the definition of making something that works for the whole family: I'm such a sucker for mushrooms and a creamy mushroom chicken is my absolute comfort food, and my kids love rice and chicken (and honestly, they just eat around the mushrooms). Cooking the rice right in the broth and coconut milk makes it so flavorful and rich! This would be incredible with skin-on bone-in chicken thighs if you're into that, but no matter what, this is a cozy dish I come back to again and again.

CHICKEN

1 pound boneless, skinless chicken breasts, cut widthwise into 4- to 5-inch pieces

1 teaspoon kosher salt

¼ teaspoon freshly ground black pepper

1 tablespoon all-purpose flour, gluten-free if needed

2 tablespoons extra-virgin olive oil

CREAMY MUSHROOM RICE

1 tablespoon extra-virgin olive oil

1 small shallot, minced

4 garlic cloves, minced

8 ounces cremini mushrooms, sliced (about 3 cups)

1 tablespoon minced fresh thyme

Kosher salt and freshly ground black pepper

1½ cups basmati rice

3 cups chicken stock or bone broth, plus more as needed

1 (13.5-ounce) can full-fat coconut milk

Grated Parmesan cheese, for serving

MAKE THE CHICKEN: In a large, shallow bowl, add the **chicken** and season on all sides with the **salt** and **pepper**. Sprinkle the **flour** over the chicken and toss to coat. Set aside.

In a large Dutch oven or heavy, lidded pot over medium heat, heat **the olive oil**. Add the dredged chicken pieces and cook until the underside begins to crisp, about 5 minutes. Reduce the heat to medium-low. Flip and cook until the chicken is cooked to 165°F and is golden brown, another 5 minutes. Remove the pot from the heat. Transfer the cooked chicken to a plate and set aside.

MAKE THE CREAMY MUSHROOM RICE: In the same pot over medium heat, heat the **oil**. Add the **shallot** and **garlic** and cook, stirring, until fragrant, 1 to 2 minutes. Add the **mushrooms** and **thyme** and cook, stirring, until the liquid in the mushrooms has cooked out, about 5 minutes. Season generously with **salt** and **pepper** and continue cooking, stirring occasionally, until the mushrooms are firm and starting to brown on the edges, another 5 minutes. Transfer about half of the mushrooms to the plate with the chicken.

Add the **rice** to the pot and stir until toasty and fragrant, 1 minute. Stir in the **stock** and **coconut milk** and bring the mixture to a boil. Reduce the heat to medium-low, cover, and cook until the rice is tender, about 20 minutes. Return the reserved chicken and mushrooms to the pot and stir to warm through. Taste and adjust the seasoning as needed, and feel free to cook for a few extra minutes to help the rice thicken, if desired, or add a splash of water or stock if you'd like it more saucy. Remove the pot from the heat.

Serve hot, topped with grated **Parmesan**.

Chicken Parmesan–Stuffed Sweet Potatoes

SERVES 4

Gluten free
Nut free

I first shared a stuffed sweet potato recipe on Instagram in 2024, with sort of a taco/burrito vibe. To be honest, it wasn't very photogenic, so I didn't think it would do all that well. But to my surprise, it went viral with millions of views. People loved it (and shared my appreciation for fugly dinner ideas)! So I thought, what else can I stuff into a sweet potato? Of course, my first thought was about my kids, who love anything with cheese and red sauce. And since sweet potatoes are such a versatile vehicle for whatever flavors you want, I put together this recipe and it's shockingly good! If you're not into sweet potatoes, you can use a big russet potato and follow the same instructions.

4 medium sweet potatoes

1 tablespoon extra-virgin olive oil, plus more for the sweet potatoes

1 small yellow onion, diced

4 garlic cloves, minced

1 teaspoon Italian seasoning

½ teaspoon kosher salt

½ teaspoon freshly ground black pepper

2 cups shredded Jordan's Foolproof Spatchcock Chicken (page 109), rotisserie chicken, or 2 large, cooked chicken breasts, shredded

2 cups marinara sauce

1 cup shredded mozzarella cheese

¼ cup grated Parmesan cheese

¼ cup fresh basil leaves, roughly chopped, plus more for serving

Preheat the oven to 425°F. Line a baking sheet with parchment paper and set aside.

Pierce each **sweet potato** several times with a fork and rub a small amount of **oil** all over the potatoes. Place them on the prepared baking sheet and bake until easily pierced with a fork or paring knife, 50 to 65 minutes, depending on your potatoes. Set aside to let cool.

In a large skillet over medium-high heat, heat the olive oil. Add the **onion** and cook, stirring, until softened, about 5 minutes. Add the **garlic**, **Italian seasoning**, **salt**, and **pepper** and cook until just fragrant, about 1 minute. Reduce the heat to medium-low and add the **chicken** and **marinara**, folding gently to combine. Cook, stirring occasionally, until the chicken is warmed through, about 3 minutes. Remove the pan from the heat and stir in ¼ cup of the **mozzarella**, plus the **Parmesan** and **basil**.

Cut open the sweet potatoes lengthwise, leaving one edge attached. Use a fork to loosen and fluff the sweet potato flesh. Divide the chicken mixture among the opened sweet potatoes and top with the remaining mozzarella. Return the stuffed sweet potatoes to the oven until the cheese is melted, about 5 minutes.

Top with more basil and serve.

WAYS TO SERVE

- Evergreen Lemony Parmesan Kale Salad *(page 59)*
- Better than Fresh, Frozen Broccoli in the Oven *(page 221)*
- Caesar Salad *(page 60)*

Four-Ingredient Baked Parmesan-Crusted Chicken Nuggets

SERVES 4 TO 6

Gluten free

Listen, the name says it all. These things are like four ingredients; they're a little cheesy, crispy, and so satisfying. Chicken nuggets are truly a staple in our house in any form, and though I'd be lying if I told you I didn't buy the ones in the frozen aisle too, sometimes; these are so fast and easy that we eat them just as often as the bagged ones! They are great on top of a salad or next to some easy roasted veggies. Bonus if you're serving these with my DIY Ketchup (page 225) for the kids, but personally I'm obsessed with dipping them in Better-than-the-Restaurant Special Sauce (page 226) or a honey mustard vibe.

1 pound boneless, skinless chicken breasts

Kosher salt and freshly ground black pepper

2 large eggs

1¼ cups grated Parmesan cheese (yes, it's a good amount of cheeze, please!)

¾ cup almond flour

Avocado oil spray

Preheat the oven to 375°F. Line a baking sheet with parchment paper and set aside.

Place the **chicken** on a cutting board and thoroughly pat dry with a paper towel. Cut the chicken into 2-inch cubes and season generously with **salt** and **pepper**. Set aside.

In a wide, shallow bowl, crack the **eggs** and beat lightly. In another wide, shallow bowl, add the **Parmesan** and **almond flour** and use a fork to combine. Set the prepared baking sheet next to the bowls.

Using tongs, a fork, or clean (or gloved) hands, dip a piece of chicken into the eggs and coat thoroughly. Shake off any excess egg and place the chicken in the Parmesan mixture. Press it gently into the mixture on all sides to coat well. Add the chicken to the prepared baking sheet and repeat with the remaining chicken.

Lightly spray the coated chicken pieces with **avocado oil**. Bake until the undersides are golden brown, 10 to 12 minutes. Flip the chicken pieces and spray lightly once more with avocado oil. Cook until the chicken has reached 165°F, another 10 to 12 minutes.

Let the chicken nuggets cool briefly and serve with your favorite dipping sauces. We love DIY Ketchup (page 225), Too-Easy-Not-to-Make Ranch Dressing (page 226), or barbecue sauce!

WAYS TO SERVE

- Caesar Salad *(page 60)*
- Better than Fresh, Frozen Broccoli in the Oven *(page 221)*
- Chop-Chop Greek Salad *(page 63)*

Lemon Parmesan Chicken Meatballs

with Garlicky Lemon Pasta

FREEZER-FRIENDLY (MEATBALLS)

SERVES 4

Gluten free
Nut free

This one goes out to my mother-in-law, who is truly like a second mother to me. I lived with my (then-future) in-laws before Jordan and I were even engaged so we could save money after college, and it really brought us so close. She is so warm and inviting, and has treated me like a daughter since day one. She makes the best-ever chicken meatballs, and I feel like sharing this recipe with you means you can experience some of her warmth, love, and amazing cooking! She has always worked seven days a week, and still somehow made dinner for her family. Her cooking is all about convenience that's still delicious. This my personal favorite way to do "spaghetti and meatballs," because it's light yet cozy and packs in veggies and protein in one beautiful dish.

MEATBALLS

- 1 pound ground chicken
- ½ cup grated Parmesan cheese
- ⅓ cup DIY Breadcrumbs (page 223), almond flour, or store-bought breadcrumbs
- 1 large egg
- 1 large shallot, minced
- 2 garlic cloves, minced
- 2 tablespoons finely chopped fresh basil leaves
- 1 tablespoon avocado or extra-virgin olive oil
- Grated zest of ½ lemon (or the whole lemon if you really love lemon flavor!)
- ¾ teaspoon kosher salt
- Freshly ground black pepper

GARLICKY LEMON PASTA

- 8 ounces spaghetti or linguine
- 3 tablespoons unsalted butter
- 1 large shallot, minced
- 2 garlic cloves, minced
- Grated zest and juice of 1 lemon, plus more for serving
- ½ cup chopped Tuscan or curly kale
- ½ cup grated Parmesan cheese, plus more for serving
- Chicken or vegetable stock, or water, as needed
- Lemon wedges, for serving (optional)

recipe continues

MAKE THE MEATBALLS: Preheat the oven to 400°F. Line a baking sheet with parchment paper and set aside.

In a large bowl, add the **ground chicken**, **Parmesan**, **breadcrumbs**, **egg**, **shallot**, **garlic**, **basil**, **avocado oil**, **lemon zest**, **salt**, and **pepper** to taste. Using your hands (I like using food-handling gloves for this), gently combine until the mixture is uniform.

Using a portioning scoop or your hands, roll the mixture into about 20 meatballs and add them to the prepared baking sheet.

Bake until the meatballs are lightly golden and reach an internal temperature of 165°F, 20 to 25 minutes.

MAKE THE PASTA: In a large pot, cook the **pasta** in well-salted boiling water according to the package directions. Remove the pot from the heat, drain the pasta, and set aside.

Return the pot to medium heat and add the **butter**. When the butter is melted, add the **shallot**, **garlic**, and **lemon zest** and cook, stirring frequently, until fragrant, barely 1 minute. Add the **kale** and cook, stirring occasionally, until the kale is slightly wilted, 3 to 5 minutes. Remove the pot from the heat.

Add the drained pasta and **lemon juice** to the pot and toss to combine. Add the **Parmesan** and toss again to coat. If you'd like to loosen up the pasta or just make it a little saucier, add a splash or two of stock or water and toss again.

Divide the pasta among bowls and top with the meatballs, extra Parmesan, and a squeeze of **lemon** if desired.

Skillet Chicken Enchiladas *with a Street Corn Twist*

SERVES 4 TO 6

Gluten free
Nut free

WE'RE MAKING ENCHILADAS, BABY! This skillet is basically a mashup of everything my family loves. My husband is obsessed with everything street corn, always grilling corn with all the fixings, and of course my kids love anything tortilla/taco adjacent. It's such a fun, colorful dish, it comes together quickly, and anytime you're broiling something cheesy on top of a skillet, people feel loved and cozy and taken care of. You can honestly double this, put it in a casserole dish to take to a party, and have people scoop it up with tortilla chips!

1½ pounds boneless, skinless chicken breasts or thighs, cut into 1-inch pieces

3 tablespoons extra-virgin olive oil

1 tablespoon store-bought taco seasoning, plus more if you want more spice

Kosher salt and freshly ground black pepper

1 medium yellow onion, chopped

2 medium bell peppers (any color), chopped

2½ cups store-bought mild red or green enchilada sauce

6 (8-inch) flour or almond flour tortillas, cut into 1-inch strips

2 cups frozen sweet corn, thawed

1½ cups shredded cheddar or Mexican cheese blend, plus more for serving

½ cup diced tomatoes (fresh or canned and drained)

½ cup (4 ounces) plain cream cheese, room temperature

¼ cup plain Greek yogurt

2 tablespoons chopped fresh chives

¼ teaspoon chili powder (optional)

Chopped fresh cilantro leaves, for serving

Super-Quick Guacamole (page 64), or sliced avocado, for serving

Lime wedges, for serving

Preheat the oven to 400°F.

In a large bowl, toss the **chicken** with 1 tablespoon of the **oil**, the **taco seasoning**, and **salt** and **pepper** to taste. Set aside.

In a large cast-iron or other oven-safe skillet over medium-high heat, heat another tablespoon of oil. Working in batches to avoid crowding the pan, add the chicken and cook, stirring or shaking the pan occasionally, until seared on all sides, about 8 minutes. (The chicken doesn't need to be fully cooked through; it's getting baked in the enchilada mixture later.) Transfer the seared chicken to a plate and repeat with the remaining chicken.

In the same pan over medium-high heat, heat the remaining tablespoon of oil. Add the **onion** and **bell peppers**, plus **salt** and **pepper** to taste, and cook, scraping up any flavorful browned bits from the chicken, until the vegetables are tender, 5 to 7 minutes. Remove the pan from the heat.

Add the **enchilada sauce** and **tortilla strips** to the skillet and toss to coat the tortilla strips thoroughly. Add the chicken and toss again to coat. Set aside.

In a medium bowl, add the **corn**, half of the **shredded cheese**, the **tomatoes**, **cream cheese**, **yogurt**, **chives**, and **chili powder** (if using). Stir well to combine. Spread the corn mixture on top of the enchiladas and top with the remaining shredded cheese.

Bake until the cheese has melted and the enchiladas are bubbly, 15 to 20 minutes.

Serve warm, topped with **cilantro**, **guacamole**, and a squeeze of **lime**.

Jordan's Foolproof Spatchcock Chicken

SERVES 4

Gluten free
Dairy Free
Nut free

Yep, this recipe made it into the book! We have been making this exact chicken dish for years. It has made its way to our holiday dinner table, many of your dinner tables, our meal-prep rotation, and now it's here in *More, Please!* If you love a rotisserie chicken (same), then this is about to be your new go-to. I love roasted chicken (those who have my first book know this!), and once we started spatchcocking it, we never went back. It cuts the cook time in half! Oh, and the marinade? SO GOOD. If you have time to marinate the chicken ahead of time, great, but nine times out of ten, I don't have more than maybe thirty minutes, and it's still perfectly delicious.

3 tablespoons extra-virgin olive oil

2 tablespoons Italian seasoning

1 tablespoon Dijon mustard

Juice of ½ lemon

2 garlic cloves, minced

1 teaspoon apple cider vinegar

1 teaspoon kosher salt

1 teaspoon onion powder

1 whole (3- to 4-pound) chicken, pasture-raised if possible

Line a baking sheet with parchment paper, set a wire rack on the baking sheet, and set aside.

In a small bowl, whisk together the **oil**, **Italian seasoning**, **Dijon**, **lemon juice**, **garlic**, **vinegar**, **salt**, and **onion powder** until smooth. Set aside.

Pat the **chicken** completely dry with paper towels and place it on a cutting board breast side down. Turn the chicken so the open cavity is facing you. Using sharp kitchen shears, cut on either side of the backbone to remove it. (You can discard the backbone or freeze it for future chicken stock.) Turn the chicken over. Place your palms over the center of the breastbone and press down firmly—this is key for the chicken to lay flat.

Place the chicken breast side up onto the prepared rack. Using clean hands or a brush, coat the chicken all over and inside the cavity with the marinade. Let the chicken marinate for up to 1 hour at room temperature. (You can roast it right away, though, if you don't have time!)

Preheat the oven to 450°F.

Roast the chicken for 15 minutes. Reduce the oven temperature to 400°F and continue roasting until the internal temperature reads 165°F, about 45 minutes. Let the chicken rest for 10 to 15 minutes before carving.

WAYS TO SERVE

- Better than Fresh, Frozen Broccoli in the Oven *(page 221)*
- The Most Underrated Nourishing Lentil Rice Bowls *(page 67)*
- Chop-Chop Greek Salad *(page 63)*

PREP TIP

Cooking for a large group, or want to make sure you've got leftovers? DOUBLE UP! Make two chickens! Go wild!

Any-Salad Pizza *with a (Stay with Me Here) Chicken Crust?!?*

SERVES 4 TO 6

Gluten free
Nut free

About ten years ago, we went to a restaurant in Manhattan that made a chicken Parmesan pizza where the base was essentially an enormous chicken cutlet instead of a traditional pizza crust. I wanted to re-create this concept, but in a way that made it a) family-friendly, b) gluten-free, and c) not quite so heavy, so this unique pizza was born! I know the chicken crust might be hard to wrap your mind around, but once you try it, I think you'll find it's an ideal base for really any salad in this book (or your own faves!). You can also go a true pizza route and top this with tomato sauce, cheese, and any other toppings.

Nonstick cooking spray
1 pound ground chicken
½ cup grated Parmesan cheese
1 teaspoon garlic powder
1 teaspoon dried oregano
½ teaspoon kosher salt
About 6 cups any favorite dressed salad, such as Chop-Chop Greek Salad (page 63), Crispy Chicken Caesar Salad (page 60), or Evergreen Lemony Parmesan Kale Salad (page 59)

Preheat the oven to 425°F. Line a baking sheet with parchment paper, spray the parchment with cooking spray, and set aside.

In a medium bowl, add the **chicken**, **Parmesan**, **garlic powder**, **oregano**, and **salt** and mix well with your hands (I like to use food-handling gloves here) to combine. Add the mixture to the prepared baking sheet and spread it evenly into a 12-inch circle. If you like, you can place another piece of parchment over the chicken and use a rolling pin to flatten it. Just make sure to remove the top layer of parchment before baking.

Bake the crust until the edges are golden and the chicken is cooked to 165°F, about 30 minutes. Let the crust cool for at least 15 minutes (this is a good time to prep your salad).

While it's still slightly warm, top the pizza crust with the **salad**, cut into wedges, and serve.

PREP TIP

If the chicken feels too sticky or wet, add a tablespoon or two of almond flour to help bind the mixture and make it easier to handle.

SABRE
PARIS

WHAT TO DO WITH A POUND OF GRO

UNDMEAT

Any Night Taco Bar
with the Best Taco Meat

SERVES 4 TO 6

Gluten-free friendly
Nut free

I love a taco bar for dinner because the meat is the only thing I actually have to think about! People can build tacos or bowls however they like, and this taco meat recipe is one of my absolute ride-or-dies. It's even something you can make on its own and keep on hand for any kind of meal prep: you can put it in baked tacos (basically quesadillas), make Our Go-To Nacho Night Nachos (page 165), add it to your eggs—the possibilities are endless. The green chilies are the secret star here! They're mild, but they add such great flavor and moisture, especially if you're using a meat that can be on the dry side, like ground chicken or turkey. If you're feeding a crowd, double this recipe. I always do (because, again, three hungry boys). And the DIY taco seasoning is truly perfection, if I do say so myself. I debate jarring it and selling it.

TACO MEAT

- 1 tablespoon extra-virgin olive oil
- 1 small yellow onion, diced
- 3 garlic cloves, minced
- 1 pound ground chicken, turkey, or beef
- Kosher salt and freshly ground black pepper
- 1 (4.5-ounce) can chopped green chilies
- ½ teaspoon ground cumin
- ½ teaspoon smoked paprika
- ½ teaspoon dried oregano
- ¼ teaspoon onion powder
- ¼ cup chopped fresh cilantro leaves (optional)
- Juice of ½ lime

FOR SERVING

- Warmed soft tortillas or taco shells
- Shredded lettuce
- Diced tomatoes
- Pickled Red Onions (page 116) or diced red onion
- Shredded cheddar cheese
- Diced avocados
- Mild jarred salsa
- Plain Greek yogurt (we love to use this just like sour cream), or sour cream
- Chopped fresh cilantro leaves
- Lime wedges
- Tortilla chips
- Cilantro-Lime Rice (page 214) (optional)

MAKE THE TACO MEAT: In a large skillet over medium heat, heat the **oil**. Add the **onion** and cook, stirring frequently, until translucent, 3 to 5 minutes. Add the **garlic** and cook until just fragrant, another minute. Add the **ground meat** and season with **salt** and **pepper**. Cook, stirring frequently and breaking up the meat with the back of a spoon or spatula, until cooked through, about 5 minutes. Drain and discard any excess fat from the pan. Stir in the **green chilies**, **cumin**, **smoked paprika**, **oregano**, and **onion powder** and taste and adjust seasoning. Remove the pan from the heat. Stir in the **cilantro** (if using) and **lime juice** and set aside.

SERVE: Add desired fixings and toppings to small bowls and set up bar-style, if you like. Fill tortillas with the taco meat and top as desired.

I Absolutely Love You, Lamb & Feta Smashburgers

MAKES 4 BURGERS

Gluten-free friendly
Nut free

If I could eat something every day forever, it would be these. I was pescatarian for a time, and when I started eating meat again, lamb was the first meat I came back to and I just love the flavor. The feta in the burgers gives you that creamy, salty hit, and the pickled red onions? I don't eat a burger without them anymore. All the flavors together are basically my dream come true. Now, I know lamb can be polarizing. Most people either love it or hate it, but if you're on the fence, these burgers might make you a convert. And as for kids: I always think of my mother-in-law, who told me very factually when I started my kids on solids, "Babies love lamb!" Sure enough, my kids all loved it and still do.

PICKLED RED ONIONS AND CUCUMBERS

- 1 medium red onion, thinly sliced (about 2 cups)
- 3 Persian or baby cucumbers, thinly sliced (about 2 cups)
- 1½ cups distilled white vinegar, plus more as needed
- 1 teaspoon kosher salt
- 1 teaspoon coconut sugar

YOGURT TZATZIKI SAUCE

- ½ cup plain Greek yogurt
- 2 Persian or baby cucumbers, grated and moisture squeezed out
- 2 garlic cloves, minced
- 2 tablespoons chopped fresh dill
- 1 tablespoon extra-virgin olive oil
- Grated zest and juice of 1 lemon

WAYS TO SERVE

- Lemon-Parsley Rice *(page 214)*
- Chop-Chop Greek Salad *(page 63)*
- My Go-To Japanese Sweet Potato Wedges *(page 217)*

LAMB BURGERS

- 1 pound ground lamb
- ½ cup crumbled feta cheese
- 2 garlic cloves, minced
- ½ teaspoon ground cumin
- ½ teaspoon ground cinnamon
- ½ teaspoon kosher salt
- Freshly ground black pepper

FOR SERVING

- 4 buns, pita breads, or lettuce wraps
- Sliced avocado
- Kalamata olives
- Sliced tomatoes
- Creamy, Better-than-Store-Bought Hummus (page 222), or store-bought hummus
- Pickled Red Onions and Cucumbers
- Creamy, Pour-It-on-Everything Feta Sauce (page 226)

MAKE THE PICKLED ONIONS AND CUCUMBERS: Place the **onion slices** in a colander and rinse them under hot water. This step is optional, but helps mellow the sharpness of the onion. Drain well.

Pack the sliced onions and **cucumbers** in a clean quart jar and add the **vinegar**, **salt**, and **coconut sugar**. Add more vinegar if needed to make sure the vegetables are fully submerged. Seal the jar tightly and shake well. Chill the pickled vegetables in the fridge for at least 30 minutes and up to overnight—the flavor improves with time! Store in the fridge for up to 1 week.

MAKE THE YOGURT TZATZIKI: In a medium bowl, add the **yogurt**, **cucumbers**, **garlic**, **dill**, **oil**, **lemon zest**, and **lemon juice** and stir to combine. Cover and chill until the burgers are ready.

MAKE THE LAMB BURGERS: In a large bowl, add the **ground lamb**, **feta**, **garlic**, **cumin**, **cinnamon**, **salt**, and **pepper** to taste. Use a silicone spatula or your hands (I like to use food-handling gloves here) to gently combine, trying not to overmix. Divide the mixture into quarters and form each quarter into a patty. Add the patty to a plate and repeat with the remaining lamb mixture.

Heat a dry, large cast-iron or nonstick skillet over medium-high heat. Add the lamb patties (they'll release their own fat quickly, which is why you don't need to grease the pan), working in batches if needed to avoid crowding. Use a spatula or grill press to smash down the patties and create thin edges. Cook until the burgers reach your desired doneness, usually 2 to 3 minutes per side for thin burgers. Remove the pan from the heat.

SERVE: Add the burgers to toasted **buns** and top with the **yogurt tzatziki**, **pickled onions and cucumbers**, and any other desired toppings.

Chimichurri Meatballs with Crazy-Good Feta Cream Sauce

SERVES 4 TO 6

Gluten free

FREEZER-FRIENDLY (MEATBALLS)

These are consistently a hit in my house, and I think it's because they truly have something for everyone. I am forever obsessed with meatballs, as you may know, and chimichurri is my husband's all-time favorite condiment. He uses it as a marinade, a sauce for veggies, pretty much anything. Here, we throw a spoonful of the chimichurri in the meat mixture for added flavor, then double down by using it for dipping alongside that amazing feta sauce. The meatballs are an easy appetizer idea and a great finger food for kids, and if they prefer ketchup or barbecue sauce, it's cool! As long as my kids eat the protein, I don't mind what sauce they're using. Serve these with any salad or just some easy flatbread, rice, or quinoa.

MEATBALLS

- 1 pound ground beef
- ⅓ cup almond flour
- 1 large egg
- 2 tablespoons Delectable Chimichurri Sauce (page 227), or 1 tablespoon extra-virgin olive oil
- 1 teaspoon kosher salt
- ½ teaspoon freshly ground black pepper
- ½ teaspoon garlic powder

FOR SERVING

- Delectable Chimichurri Sauce (page 227)
- Creamy, Pour-It-on-Everything Feta Sauce (page 226)
- Creamy, Better-than-Store-Bought Hummus (page 222)

MAKE THE MEATBALLS: Preheat the oven to 400°F. Line a baking sheet with parchment paper and set aside.

In a large bowl, add the **ground beef**, **almond flour**, **egg**, **chimichurri sauce**, **salt**, **pepper**, and **garlic powder**. Use a silicone spatula or your hands (I like to use food-handling gloves here) to gently combine, trying not to overmix. Using a spoon or small scoop, portion the meat mixture into 16 to 18 (1-inch) balls. Use your hands to roll each portion into a smooth meatball and place on the prepared baking sheet. Repeat with the remaining meat mixture, spacing the meatballs about 1 inch apart.

Bake until the meatballs reach an internal temperature of 165°F and are slightly golden around the edges, 16 to 20 minutes. Set aside.

SERVE the meatballs either layered with the **chimichurri** and **feta sauce** or with the sauces on the side for dipping.

WAYS TO SERVE

- 2-for-1 Herby Rice *(page 214)*
- My Go-To Japanese Sweet Potato Wedges *(page 217)*
- Absolutely the Best-Ever Italian Pasta Salad *(page 144)*

Delish Saucy Cheesy Pizza Burger Night!!

SERVES 4 TO 6

Gluten-free friendly
Nut free

This recipe was inspired by all the odds and ends that always seem to be hanging around in my kitchen: English muffins, the end of a jar of marinara, and usually a pound of ground meat somewhere in the fridge or freezer. I adore English muffins of any kind! I try to grab sprouted ones when possible, and gluten-free for my husband. Something about these always gives me after-school-snack vibes, so they're fun to spin into an easy, casual dinner. (And honestly, who doesn't love anything with bubbly, melted cheese on top?) Serve these with any low-effort veggies for the easiest weeknight dinner ever.

- 1 tablespoon extra-virgin olive oil
- 1 small yellow onion, diced
- 1 pound ground beef
- 2 teaspoons Italian seasoning
- 1 teaspoon kosher salt
- ½ teaspoon garlic powder
- ¼ teaspoon freshly ground black pepper
- 1 cup marinara sauce
- 4 to 6 English muffins, split
- 1 cup shredded mozzarella cheese
- Chopped fresh basil leaves, for serving (optional)

Line a baking sheet with parchment paper and set aside.

In a large skillet over medium-high heat, heat the **oil**. Add the **onion** and cook, stirring occasionally, until softened, about 5 minutes. Add the **ground beef**, **Italian seasoning**, **salt**, **garlic powder**, and **pepper** and cook, breaking up the meat with a wooden spoon or meat masher, until cooked through and beginning to crisp, about 7 minutes. Stir in the **marinara** and cook until slightly thickened, about 3 minutes. Remove the pan from the heat.

Place an oven rack in the middle of the oven and heat the broiler to high.

Place the **English muffins** cut side up on the prepared baking sheet. Toast on the middle rack until lightly browned, about 5 minutes. Divide the marinara mixture among the toasted muffins and top with the **shredded mozzarella**. Return to the oven and broil again until the cheese is just melted, about 2 minutes.

Top with fresh **basil**, if desired, and serve.

WAYS TO SERVE

- No-Fryer-Added French Fries *(page 218)*
- Evergreen Lemony Parmesan Kale Salad *(page 59)*
- Better than Fresh, Frozen Broccoli in the Oven *(page 221)*

SAFE SWAP

Don't have English muffins? Sub your go-to bagel or toast!

One-Skillet Cheesy Chicken Broccoli Rice Casserole

SERVES 4 TO 6

Gluten free
Nut free

FREEZER-FRIENDLY

Calling all broccoli-cheddar lovers! This one-skillet wonder will be on repeat in your kitchen. It checks all the boxes on flavor, nutrition, and convenience. It's hearty, nourishing, and when cheese and rice are involved, you know the fam is going to love it. This also reheats beautifully, so it's great to make ahead for a busy week, or even freeze right in the casserole dish and pop in the oven another time.

2 tablespoons extra-virgin olive oil

1 pound ground chicken

Kosher salt and freshly ground black pepper

1 small yellow onion, finely chopped

2 garlic cloves, minced

½ teaspoon paprika

½ teaspoon dried parsley

1½ cups basmati rice

2 cups chicken stock or bone broth

3 cups roughly chopped broccoli florets

2 cups shredded sharp cheddar cheese

½ cup milk of choice (dairy or nondairy)

In a large, oven-safe skillet over medium-high heat, add 1 tablespoon of the **oil**. Add the **chicken**, season with **salt** and **pepper**, and cook, stirring frequently, until the chicken is cooked through, about 7 minutes. Remove the pan from the heat and transfer the chicken to a plate.

Return the pan to medium-high heat and add the remaining tablespoon of oil. Add the **onion** and cook, stirring frequently, until soft and translucent, about 5 minutes. Add the **garlic**, **paprika**, and **parsley** and cook until just fragrant, about 30 seconds. Add the chicken back to the skillet, plus the **rice**, **chicken stock**, and **2 cups of water**. Stir to combine, increase the heat to high, and bring to a boil. Reduce the heat to low, cover, and cook, undisturbed, for 10 minutes. Add the **broccoli** and stir to combine. Cover the pan again and continue cooking, stirring occasionally, until the rice and broccoli are fully cooked, 10 to 12 minutes. Remove the pan from the heat.

While the rice cooks, preheat the oven to 425°F.

Add 1 cup of the **cheddar**, plus the **milk**, to the rice mixture and fold until combined. Top with the remaining cup of cheddar. Bake until the cheese is melted and bubbly, 5 to 7 minutes. Serve hot.

Juicy Caramelized Onion Turkey Burgers

SERVES 4

Gluten-free friendly
Dairy-free friendly

FREEZER-FRIENDLY

My mom and dad live in "farmland," as they like to say, about 45 minutes from us, surrounded by beautiful farms. One nearby farm sells these caramelized onion turkey burgers that I honestly dream about. Now, we do get these burgers every time we go out to see my parents, but they now spend about 80 percent of the year in Florida. So of course, I had to figure out my own homemade version. These redeem the sad reputation of the dry turkey burger: they're juicy, flavorful, and the caramelized onions really shine. You can keep things simple and do lettuce, tomato, and pickles, or maybe get fancy and add Gruyère (amazing with the sweet onions), or make the Creamy, Pour-It-on-Everything Feta Sauce (page 226) to dollop on top.

TURKEY BURGERS

- 1 pound ground turkey
- ½ cup chopped Simply Perfect Caramelized Onions (page 222)
- 3 garlic cloves, minced
- 2 tablespoons chopped fresh parsley leaves
- 2 tablespoons chopped scallions (white and light green parts)
- 1 tablespoon plain Greek yogurt or mayonnaise
- 1 tablespoon Dijon mustard
- 1 teaspoon kosher salt
- ¼ teaspoon freshly ground black pepper
- 2 tablespoons extra-virgin olive oil

FOR SERVING

- Hamburger buns or lettuce wraps
- Sliced cheese (I love Swiss or Gruyère with these burgers)
- Pickled Red Onions (page 116)
- Sliced avocado
- Pickles
- DIY Ketchup (page 225), or ketchup of choice
- Creamy, Better-than-Store-Bought Hummus (page 222)
- Creamy, Pour-It-on-Everything Feta Sauce (page 226)
- Mustard
- Mayonnaise

MAKE THE BURGERS: In a medium bowl, add the **ground turkey**, **onions**, **garlic**, **parsley**, **scallions**, **yogurt**, **Dijon**, **salt**, and **pepper** and use a silicone spatula or your hands (I like using food-handling gloves here) to combine. Shape the mixture into 4 patties and set aside.

In a large skillet over medium heat, heat the **oil**. Add the patties to the skillet and cook until the underside is golden brown, about 5 minutes. Flip and cook the burgers until an internal thermometer reads 165°F, another 5 minutes or so. Remove the pan from the heat.

SERVE: Make these into lettuce wraps or old-school burgers with all of your favorite toppings.

WAYS TO SERVE

- Evergreen Lemony Parmesan Kale Salad *(page 59)*
- My Go-To Japanese Sweet Potato Wedges *(page 217)*
- Chop-Chop Greek Salad *(page 63)*

Cheeseburger Bowls
with Special Sauce

SERVES 4

Gluten free
Nut free

Another family favorite that basically evolved from trying to re-create my kids' restaurant favorites at home in a slightly more balanced, maybe-get-a-veggie-in format! My five-year-old *loves* cheeseburgers and orders them at pretty much every restaurant. These bowls are a way to mix it up a bit and let each person build their own bowl with their own preference of toppings. I make this with beef, but you can do it with ground turkey, chicken, or a plant-based alternative. And normally I'd say "you do you" with the condiments, but in all seriousness, the Special Sauce truly ties the whole thing together. It's a must!

ROASTED SWEET POTATOES

- 2 large sweet potatoes, cut into ½-inch cubes (can also use russet potatoes)
- 2 tablespoons avocado or extra-virgin olive oil
- Kosher salt and freshly ground black pepper

BURGER MEAT

- Avocado or extra-virgin olive oil
- 1 pound ground beef
- ½ teaspoon kosher salt
- ¼ teaspoon garlic powder
- ¼ teaspoon onion powder
- ¼ teaspoon smoked paprika
- Freshly ground black pepper

BOWLS

- Shredded cheddar cheese
- Shredded lettuce
- Diced tomatoes
- Diced pickles
- Sliced avocado
- Sliced jalapeños
- Sesame seeds
- Better-than-the-Restaurant Special Sauce (page 226)
- Simply Perfect Caramelized Onions (page 222)
- DIY Ketchup (page 225)

MAKE THE SWEET POTATOES: Preheat the oven to 425°F. Line a baking sheet with parchment paper and set aside.

In a large bowl, add the **sweet potatoes**, **oil**, and **salt** and **pepper** to taste and toss well to coat. Add the sweet potatoes to the prepared baking sheet and spread them out in an even layer. Roast until the edges begin to caramelize, about 30 minutes. Flip the potatoes and continue cooking until slightly crisp, 10 to 15 minutes more. Set aside to cool slightly.

MAKE THE BURGER MEAT: In a large skillet over medium heat, heat the **oil**. Add the **ground beef**, **salt**, **garlic powder**, **onion powder**, **smoked paprika**, and **pepper** to taste. Use a wooden spoon or meat masher (my fave) to break up the meat and continue cooking, stirring occasionally, until the meat is browned, 6 to 8 minutes. Remove the pan from the heat.

ASSEMBLE THE BOWLS: Divide the sweet potatoes and burger meat among bowls. Build your bowl with any desired toppings and drizzle generously with the **Special Sauce**.

One-Pot Creamy Swedish Meatballs *(Like Mom Used to Make!)*

FREEZER-FRIENDLY (MEATBALLS)

SERVES 4 TO 6

Gluten-free friendly

Calling all comfort food lovers! If there's one recipe in here I'd recommend for a cold, rainy, or snowy night, it's this one. You know I am a sucker for any meatball, yet somehow I hadn't done a version of Swedish meatballs until this book. This dish has everything you need: satisfying, warm-spiced meatballs, a light-yet-creamy sauce, and classic egg noodles! My one tip is not to skip the nutmeg in the meatballs; it's a hallmark of that Swedish flavor, so even though there's just a tiny bit, it makes all the difference. Cheers to more fugly food that is so darn tasty.

MEATBALLS

1 pound ground beef

½ cup almond flour

¼ cup minced yellow onion

2 large eggs

1 teaspoon kosher salt

½ teaspoon freshly ground black pepper

Pinch of ground nutmeg

2 tablespoons extra-virgin olive oil

CREAMY NOODLES

¼ cup unsalted butter or extra-virgin olive oil

¼ cup almond flour

4 cups beef stock or bone broth

1 cup full-fat coconut milk

1 teaspoon Dijon mustard

1 teaspoon kosher salt

3 cups egg noodles or short pasta, such as fusilli

1 cup frozen peas

1 cup grated Parmesan cheese, plus more for serving

1 tablespoon minced fresh parsley leaves, plus more for serving

MAKE THE MEATBALLS: In a large bowl, add the **ground beef**, **almond flour**, **onion**, **eggs**, **salt**, **pepper**, and **nutmeg**. Use a silicone spatula or your hands to gently combine.

Using a spoon or small scoop, portion the meat mixture into about 16 (1-inch) balls. Use your hands to roll each portion into a smooth meatball and set aside on a plate. Repeat with the remaining meat mixture and set aside.

In a Dutch oven or large, heavy pot over medium heat, heat the **oil**. Working in batches to avoid crowding the pot, brown the meatballs on all sides until deeply golden, 6 to 8 minutes total. (They'll continue cooking later with the noodles, so don't worry if they're not cooked through yet.) Transfer the cooked meatballs to a clean plate and repeat with the remaining meatballs. Remove the pot from the heat.

MAKE THE NOODLES: In the same pot over medium heat, melt the **butter**. Add the **almond flour** and cook, stirring constantly, until the mixture smells a bit nutty, about 2 minutes. Add the **stock, coconut milk**, **Dijon**, and **salt** and whisk to eliminate any lumps from the almond flour. Add the uncooked **pasta** and browned meatballs and stir well to coat. Cover and cook for 5 minutes.

Add the **frozen peas** and stir to combine. Cook, leaving the lid off this time, until the pasta is tender, another 5 minutes, adding a **splash of water** as needed if the pot looks too dry. Remove the pot from the heat and stir in the **Parmesan** and **parsley**.

Serve hot, topped with additional Parmesan and parsley as desired.

Meatloaf Meatballs

with Crispy Potatoes & Peas

FREEZER-FRIENDLY (MEATBALLS)

SERVES 4 TO 6

Gluten free
Dairy free

Growing up, we had my mom's meatloaf at least twice a month. My dad loves it so much, he'll even ask for it in the middle of summer, with potatoes! But now that I'm the one making dinner for my own family, it truly comes down to whatever's easiest to feed them. For me, you know that's gonna be some form of meatball, and here it's made with the iconic flavors of a classic meatloaf. Finger food for little kids? Check. Hearty enough for adults? Check. Crispy potatoes and buttery peas on the side will make this a favorite in your house, too.

CRISPY POTATOES AND PEAS

- 1½ pounds small yellow or Yukon Gold potatoes, scrubbed and large ones cut in half
- 2 tablespoons extra-virgin olive oil
- ½ teaspoon garlic powder
- ¼ teaspoon smoked paprika
- Kosher salt and freshly ground black pepper
- 2 cups frozen green peas

MEATBALLS

- Nonstick cooking spray
- 1 pound ground beef
- ⅓ cup almond flour
- ¼ cup grated white onion
- 1 large egg
- 2 tablespoons DIY Ketchup (page 225), store-bought ketchup, or barbecue sauce
- 1 teaspoon kosher salt
- 1 teaspoon ground paprika
- ½ teaspoon garlic powder
- Barbecue sauce, for brushing and serving

MAKE THE POTATOES AND PEAS: Preheat the oven to 400°F. Line a baking sheet with parchment paper and set aside.

In a large bowl, add the **potatoes**, **oil**, **garlic powder**, **smoked paprika**, and **salt** and **pepper** to taste and toss well to coat. Add the potatoes in an even layer to the prepared baking sheet and roast for 20 minutes. Add the peas to the baking sheet, flip or nudge the potatoes to move them around a bit, and return to the oven to roast until the potatoes are tender, another 20 minutes.

MAKE THE MEATBALLS: Spray a 12-cup muffin tin with **nonstick spray** and set aside.

In a large bowl, add the **ground beef**, **almond flour**, **onion**, **egg**, **ketchup**, **salt**, **paprika**, and **garlic powder**. Using a silicone spatula or your hands (I like to use food-handling gloves), gently combine until the mixture is uniform and evenly incorporated. Divide the mixture into 12 equal-sized portions, roll into meatballs, and place each meatball in the prepared muffin tin.

Add 2 tablespoons of **barbecue sauce** to a small bowl and brush the sauce onto the meatballs. Bake the meatballs until the internal temperature reaches 165°F, about 30 minutes. (If the potatoes are already done, you can reduce the oven temperature to 350°F.)

Serve the meatballs hot with the crispy potatoes and peas on the side, with more BBQ sauce for dipping.

The Ever-Popular Thai Turkey Meatballs
with Coconut Curry
FREEZER-FRIENDLY (MEATBALLS)

SERVES 4 TO 6

Gluten-free friendly
Dairy Free
Nut free

So, there's this recipe reel I've shared on Instagram more times than I can count. Why? Because it goes viral Every. Single. Time. It's been the top recipe on my website since 2020, when I first shared it. What is it about this recipe that people love so much? I think it's the sauce: it's creamy, it's curry-ish without a lot of fuss, and everything comes together so fast. The only tricky part can be the red curry paste, because some can be pretty mild, while some can be really spicy. So check your spice level in the curry paste before you determine how much to use!

THAI MEATBALLS

- 1 pound ground turkey or chicken
- 1 cup DIY Breadcrumbs (page 223) or panko breadcrumbs
- 1 large egg
- 2 garlic cloves, minced
- 1½ tablespoons coconut aminos
- 1 teaspoon ground ginger
- 1 teaspoon red curry paste, plus more (depends on the heat level of your curry paste!)
- ½ teaspoon kosher salt
- Freshly ground black pepper

COCONUT CURRY

- 2 tablespoons avocado or extra-virgin olive oil
- 1 medium red bell pepper, sliced
- 1 small yellow onion, diced
- 1 tablespoon red curry paste, plus more (depends on the heat level of your curry paste!)
- 1 (13.5-ounce) can full-fat coconut milk
- 1 tablespoon coconut aminos
- Chopped fresh cilantro leaves, for serving

MAKE THE MEATBALLS: In a large bowl, add the **ground turkey**, **breadcrumbs**, **egg**, **garlic**, **coconut aminos**, **ginger**, **red curry paste**, **salt**, and **pepper** to taste. Use a silicone spatula or your hands (I like to use food-handling gloves here) to gently combine, trying not to overmix. Chill the mixture until firm, about 30 minutes.

Preheat the oven to 400°F. Line a baking sheet with parchment paper.

Using your hands or a cookie scoop, roll the turkey mixture into 1-inch balls and add them to the prepared baking sheet. Bake until the meatballs are golden brown and cooked to an internal temperature of 165°F, about 18 minutes.

MAKE THE COCONUT CURRY: In a large, high-sided skillet over medium-high heat, heat the **oil**. Add the **bell pepper** and **onion** and cook, stirring frequently, until the pepper is softened and the onion begins to brown, 5 to 7 minutes. Add the **curry paste** and stir to coat the vegetables, cooking until just fragrant, about 1 minute. Add the **coconut milk** and **coconut aminos** and bring the mixture to a simmer. Reduce the heat to low and simmer, stirring occasionally, until the flavors come together and the mixture is slightly thickened, at least 30 minutes and up to 1 hour. During this time, you can add the cooked meatballs and let them simmer in the sauce to boost the flavor even more. Remove the pan from the heat.

Top the curry with chopped **cilantro** and serve.

WHAT TO MAKE WITH A BOX OF

PASTA

One-Pot French Onion Soup Pasta

SERVES 4 TO 6

Gluten-free friendly
Nut free

If you love French onion soup (who doesn't?) or have tried the French onion soup meatballs from my website, words cannot describe how excited I am for you to experience this. It's cozy, savory, and cheesy, but once again, that coconut milk brings the creaminess yet still makes the dish surprisingly light. You can use any short pasta here, but I have to recommend the little shells because they trap so much flavor in each bite. Do keep an eye on the cooking time since each shape and type will vary.

- 2 tablespoons unsalted butter
- 2 tablespoons extra-virgin olive oil
- 3 large yellow onions, thinly sliced, or 2 cups Simply Perfect Caramelized Onions (page 222)
- Kosher salt and freshly ground black pepper
- 4 garlic cloves, minced
- 2 teaspoons chopped fresh thyme leaves
- 1 teaspoon Worcestershire sauce
- 1 teaspoon Dijon mustard
- ¼ cup dry white wine
- 3 cups beef or vegetable stock
- 12 ounces short pasta, such as small shells or penne
- 1 cup shredded Gruyère cheese, plus more for serving
- ¼ cup full-fat coconut milk
- Chopped fresh parsley, for serving (optional)

In a large Dutch oven or large, high-sided skillet over medium-high heat, heat the **butter** and **oil**. Add the **onions** and a big pinch of **salt** and toss to coat them in the butter and oil. Cook, stirring frequently, until the onions are translucent and beginning to brown along some edges, about 10 minutes. Reduce the heat to medium-low and continue cooking, stirring occasionally, until the onions have reduced significantly and are a deep, golden-brown color, about 45 minutes. (If you're using the caramelized onions, you can skip this step and simply warm them in the pot before proceeding.)

Increase the heat to medium-high and add the **garlic** and **thyme**. Cook, stirring frequently, until fragrant, about 2 minutes. Add the **Worcestershire** and **Dijon** and stir to combine. Add the **wine** and cook, scraping the bottom of the pot to loosen any browned bits, until the liquid has evaporated, 1 to 2 minutes. Add the **stock**, **pasta**, and **1 cup of water** and bring the mixture to a simmer. Reduce the heat to medium-low and cook according to the pasta package instructions, stirring very frequently, until most of the liquid has evaporated and the pasta is tender. (Remember that you're working with a bit less liquid here than if you were just cooking the pasta in a large pot of water, so you can add a splash of water if the pot looks dry before the pasta is cooked through.) Remove the pot from the heat.

Add the **Gruyère** and **coconut milk** and stir until the mixture is creamy and the cheese is melted. Serve topped with additional Gruyère and chopped **parsley** (if using).

Meat-Lover-Approved, Veggie-Loaded Lentil Bolognese

FREEZER-FRIENDLY

SERVES 4 TO 6 (WITH EXTRA SAUCE FOR THE FREEZER)

Gluten-free friendly
Nut free

My husband isn't Italian, but he always loves the idea of a Sunday sauce (and I mean, who doesn't?). Some versions of lentil Bolognese can end up just tasting like . . . well, lentil soup, but the wine here adds great depth of flavor, and the ground pumpkin seeds, while they might seem unusual, create a richness that makes this so satisfying. You can go traditional and serve this with any pasta, but I also love it with zucchini noodles, or a mix of zoodles and spaghetti. And this makes a big batch, so you can stash half in the freezer for future busy nights.

1 cup French green lentils
¼ cup pumpkin or sunflower seeds
2 tablespoons extra-virgin olive oil
1 large yellow onion, diced
½ cup peeled, diced carrots
½ cup diced celery
Kosher salt and freshly ground black pepper
3 garlic cloves, minced
1½ teaspoons dried oregano
1 (5.3-ounce) can tomato paste
½ cup dry red wine
3 cups chicken stock or bone broth
1 (14.5-ounce) can crushed tomatoes
1 tablespoon balsamic vinegar
12 ounces long pasta of choice, such as spaghetti or fettuccine
Grated Parmesan cheese, for serving
Chopped fresh basil leaves, for serving

In a medium bowl, cover the **lentils** with water and soak for at least 30 minutes (no more than 1 hour). Drain and set aside.

In a food processor, add the **pumpkin seeds** and pulse until finely crushed. Set aside.

In a large pot over medium-high heat, heat the **oil**. Add the **onion**, **carrots**, and **celery**, and season generously with **salt** and **pepper**. Cook, stirring occasionally, until the vegetables are softened and the onion is golden brown, 10 to 12 minutes. Add the **garlic** and **oregano** and cook until just fragrant, 1 minute. Add the **tomato paste** and reduce the heat to medium. Cook, stirring frequently, until the tomato paste is a deep red color, about 2 minutes. Stir in the **wine**, scraping up any browned bits from the bottom of the pan. Cook, stirring, until the alcohol has cooked off, about 2 minutes.

Add the **stock**, **crushed tomatoes**, lentils, and crushed pumpkin seeds and stir well to combine. Increase the heat to high and bring the mixture to a boil. Reduce the heat to medium-low and cook, stirring occasionally, until the lentils are tender, about 30 minutes. Stir in the **balsamic vinegar** and remove the pot from the heat. Taste and adjust the seasoning as desired. Transfer about half of the Bolognese to a freezer-safe container. Cover the pot to keep the remaining sauce warm.

Cook the **pasta** in a large pot of well-salted boiling water according to the package instructions. Reserve 1 cup of the pasta cooking water.

Transfer the hot pasta to the sauce and toss well to coat. Add a few splashes of pasta water as needed to help loosen the sauce.

Serve with lots of grated **Parmesan** and chopped **basil**.

Ride-or-Die No-Boil Pasta Bake

SERVES 6 TO 8

Gluten-free friendly
Nut free

FREEZER-FRIENDLY

How many times have I made this in real life? Probably hundreds. And that says a lot because for as much as I cook, it's rare that I make the same thing so many times. This is like a classic baked ziti, but reimagined to require the lowest effort possible, and works with virtually any variation you can throw at it. Use regular, gluten-free, or even chickpea pasta—it'll work. Keep it vegetarian (the cottage cheese brings great protein here), or add meat—it'll work. Dump in a jar of vodka sauce instead of the marinara—it will work! Add broccoli, peas, leftover roasted vegetables, whatever you have on hand or want to use up. This also freezes and reheats like a dream. My OG blog readers know the original recipe, but this one is somehow even better. You'll notice some tweaks and additions—I can't wait for you to try it!

1 pound penne pasta, or similar shape

2½ cups marinara sauce

1 cup full-fat coconut milk or whole milk

1 cup chicken or vegetable stock

1 cup loosely packed baby spinach or ½ cup frozen peas (optional)

1 cup cooked and seasoned meat, such as sliced Italian sausage or chopped meatballs (optional)

2 garlic cloves, minced

1 teaspoon onion powder

½ teaspoon dried oregano

Kosher salt and freshly ground black pepper

½ cup cottage cheese

1½ cups shredded mozzarella cheese

Grated Parmesan cheese, for serving

Preheat the oven to 400°F.

In a 9x13-inch baking dish, add the **pasta**, **marinara**, **milk**, **stock**, **spinach** (if using), **meat** (if using), **garlic**, **onion powder**, **oregano**, and **salt** and **pepper** to taste. Stir gently to combine. Dollop the **cottage cheese** all over and top with the **mozzarella**. Cover the dish with foil. Bake until the pasta is cooked through and the cheeses are melted, 35 to 40 minutes. Remove the foil and set the oven to broil. Broil until the cheese is bubbly and golden, about 2 minutes.

Serve hot, topped with grated **Parmesan**.

Garlicky Broccoli & Steak Lo Mein

SERVES 4 TO 6

Gluten-free friendly
Dairy free
Nut free

Growing up, when my dad was traveling for work, my mom would order takeout and let us kids—get this—eat dinner while watching TV (scandalous, right?). My order from the local spot was always a simple lo mein with some kind of protein. Nowadays, I find this garlicky broccoli and steak version takes less time to make than it would to call and wait for a takeout order. One of my favorite tips in the book is in this recipe, and that's to cook the (frozen!) broccoli right in with the noodles. It makes it so fast and convenient. If steak isn't your thing, you can always use chicken or tofu.

1 pound flank steak

Kosher salt and freshly ground black pepper

8 ounces spaghetti or other long noodle

3 cups fresh or frozen broccoli florets

1 tablespoon extra-virgin olive oil

1 small red bell pepper, thinly sliced

1 medium carrot, peeled and shredded

4 garlic cloves, minced

¼ cup coconut aminos

¼ cup coconut sugar

2 teaspoons sesame oil

¼ teaspoon ground ginger

¼ teaspoon crushed red pepper flakes (optional)

Mung bean sprouts, for serving (optional but feels fancy)

Sliced scallions, for serving (white and green parts)

Sesame seeds, for serving

With a sharp knife, slice the **steak** across the grain in ¼-inch strips. Set aside.

In a large pot of well-salted boiling water, cook the **noodles** according to the package instructions, adding the **broccoli** for the last 5 minutes of cooking time. Remove the pot from the heat. Drain the noodles and broccoli and set aside.

In a large, high-sided skillet over medium-high heat, heat the **olive oil**. Add the steak and season with **salt** and **bell pepper** and cook, stirring occasionally, until the steak is mostly cooked through but still has a bit of pink in the middle, about 5 minutes. Add the **bell pepper**, **carrot**, and **garlic** and cook, stirring frequently, until just starting to soften, another 1 to 2 minutes. Remove the pan from the heat.

In a small bowl, whisk together the **coconut aminos**, **coconut sugar**, **sesame oil**, **ginger**, **red pepper flakes** (if using), and lots of **black pepper**. Set aside.

Add the drained noodles and broccoli to the skillet with the steak and pour in the sauce. Toss well to coat. Top with the **bean sprouts** (if using), **scallions**, and **sesame seeds** and serve hot.

Absolutely the Best-Ever Italian Pasta Salad
with Shallot Vinaigrette

SERVES 6

Gluten-free friendly
Nut free

Guys, I'm probably never making another pasta salad that's not this one, and I think you'll feel the same. I was in kind of a pasta salad rut for a while when I unearthed a jar of banana peppers in my pantry. Little did I know they can make such a difference in a pasta salad! Paired with the shallots in the dressing (you know I'm obsessed with shallots), the flavors are out of this world. You can serve this at any barbecues or dinner parties, or just prep it for lunches and sides in the week ahead. My kids love this so much that I often just add some leftover chicken and there's dinner!

DRESSING

½ cup extra-virgin olive oil

¼ cup red wine vinegar

3 tablespoons minced shallots

2 garlic cloves, minced

2 teaspoons minced fresh parsley leaves

2 teaspoons dried oregano

Kosher salt and freshly ground black pepper

PASTA SALAD

1 pound short pasta, such as elbows, small shells, or fusilli

1 cup packed baby spinach or baby arugula, chopped

1 pint cherry tomatoes, halved

1 (15-ounce) can no-salt-added chickpeas, rinsed and well-drained

1 cup grated Parmesan cheese, plus more for serving

¾ cup jarred banana peppers, roughly chopped

¾ cup pitted green olives and/or kalamata olives, roughly chopped

¾ cup diced fresh mozzarella cheese or fresh mozzarella balls

½ teaspoon freshly ground black pepper

MAKE THE DRESSING: In a medium bowl, whisk together the **oil**, **vinegar**, **shallots**, **garlic**, **parsley**, **oregano**, and **salt** and **pepper** to taste. Set aside.

MAKE THE PASTA SALAD: Cook the **pasta** in a large pot of well-salted boiling water according to the package instructions. Remove the pot from the heat. Rinse the pasta in cold water and drain well.

Transfer the cooked pasta to a large bowl and add the **spinach**, **tomatoes**, **chickpeas**, **Parmesan**, **banana peppers**, **olives**, **mozzarella**, and **pepper**. Pour the dressing all over and toss well to coat. Cover and refrigerate the pasta salad for at least 1 hour for the flavors to marinate (the longer it sits, the better!).

Serve topped with additional grated Parmesan.

WAYS TO SERVE

- Jordan's Foolproof Spatchcock Chicken *(page 109)*
- Chimichurri Meatballs *(page 119)*
- Juicy Caramelized Onion Turkey Burgers *(page 124)*

One-Pot Creamy Chicken Potpie Pasta

SERVES 4 TO 6

Gluten-free friendly
Dairy-free friendly
Nut free

Something about chicken potpie just *screams* comfort food, right?! This one-pot pasta version truly is one of the best-ever twists on the flavors of a potpie. Here, I'm using coconut milk because I love the creaminess it adds, and it makes this dish dairy-free. No one in my house is dairy-free, but sometimes it's nice to switch things up. But if coconut isn't your thing, swapping in dairy milk will work just as well, I promise. And as always, I love using bone broth to pack in extra protein and nutrients. This dish really is a gem—I hope you love it as much as our family does.

2 tablespoons extra-virgin olive oil or unsalted butter

1 pound boneless, skinless chicken breasts

Kosher salt and freshly ground black pepper

2 large carrots, peeled and diced

2 large celery stalks, diced

½ medium yellow onion, diced

4 ounces cremini mushrooms, sliced (about ¾ cup)

4 garlic cloves, minced

½ teaspoon dried thyme leaves

½ teaspoon ground sage

¼ teaspoon smoked paprika

4 cups chicken stock or bone broth

2 cups full-fat coconut milk or whole milk

½ pound short pasta, such as elbows, small shells, or farfalle

1 cup frozen corn

1 cup frozen peas

2 tablespoons chopped fresh parsley leaves, plus more for serving

Crushed crackers, for serving (optional)

In a large Dutch oven or other heavy pot over medium heat, heat the **oil**. Add the **chicken** and season generously with **salt** and **pepper**. Sear the chicken until deeply golden on both sides, 3 to 5 minutes per side. Remove the pot from the heat and transfer the chicken to a plate.

Return the same pot to medium heat and add the **carrots**, **celery**, **onion**, and **mushrooms**, plus salt and pepper to taste, and cook, stirring frequently, until tender, about 10 minutes. Add the **garlic**, **thyme**, **sage**, and **smoked paprika** and cook, stirring, until fragrant, about 1 minute. Add the **chicken stock** and **coconut milk** and stir, scraping up any browned bits from the bottom of the pot. Cut the seared chicken into bite-sized chunks and add it to the pot.

Increase the heat to medium-high and bring to a boil. Add the **pasta** and reduce the heat to medium. Cook, stirring frequently, until the pasta is nearly tender, 10 to 15 minutes (depending on your pasta). Add the **corn**, **peas**, and **parsley** and continue cooking until the pasta is tender and the sauce has thickened, 6 to 8 more minutes. Remove the pot from the heat. The sauce will thicken further as the pasta cools.

Serve warm topped with additional parsley and **crushed crackers**, if you like.

One-Skillet Creamy Tomato Sausage Orzo

SERVES 4 TO 6

Gluten-free friendly
Nut free

Somehow orzo has become the forgotten pasta shape in my house, and recently I set out to change that. This is a one-skillet sausage orzo that's extra creamy (minus the cream) and comes together in less than 30 minutes. The best part? It's made with ingredients I tend to have on hand about 95 percent of the time. The full-fat coconut milk is the secret ingredient here, and no, I promise the end result will *not* taste like coconut. A reminder here that gluten-free pasta tends to absorb more liquid than traditional pasta, so if the pan is looking dry, you can always add more stock as needed.

- 2 tablespoons extra-virgin olive oil, plus more as needed
- 5 mild Italian chicken sausage links, sliced into ¼-inch pieces
- 1 cup orzo pasta
- 1 cup cherry tomatoes, halved
- 1 small yellow onion, diced
- ½ cup chopped jarred roasted red peppers
- 5 garlic cloves, minced
- 1 teaspoon smoked paprika
- ½ teaspoon Italian seasoning
- Red pepper flakes (optional)
- 1½ cups chicken stock or bone broth, plus more as needed
- Kosher salt and freshly ground black pepper
- 1 cup full-fat coconut milk or whole milk
- 1 cup packed baby spinach, chopped
- ⅓ cup marinara sauce
- Juice of ½ lemon
- Grated Parmesan cheese, for serving
- Chopped fresh basil leaves, for serving

In a Dutch oven or large, high-sided skillet over medium-high heat, heat the **oil**. Add the **chicken sausage** and cook, stirring occasionally, until the edges are a bit crispy, 7 to 10 minutes. Remove the pan from the heat. Transfer the sausage to a plate and set aside.

Return the pan to medium-high heat and add a splash more oil if needed. Add the **orzo**, **tomatoes**, **onion**, **red peppers**, **garlic**, **smoked paprika**, **Italian seasoning**, and **red pepper flakes** (if using). Cook, stirring frequently, until the mixture is fragrant and the orzo takes on some color, about 1 minute. Stir in the **stock**, plus **salt** and **pepper** to taste, and bring to a boil. Reduce the heat to medium-low and cook, stirring frequently to keep the orzo from sticking, until the orzo is nearly tender but not all the way cooked, about 10 minutes. If the pan looks dry, you can add more stock as needed.

Add the **coconut milk**, **spinach**, and **marinara** and continue cooking, stirring occasionally, until the mixture is thickened and the orzo is fully cooked, 5 to 10 more minutes. Remove the pan from the heat and add the **lemon juice**.

Serve hot, topped with the **Parmesan** and fresh **basil**.

One-Skillet Cheesy Pizza Mac & Cheese

SERVES 4 TO 6

Gluten-free friendly
Nut free

If you were to ask my middle son for his three favorite foods, he'd say: green salad, mac & cheese, and pizza. As you can imagine, we make a lot of pizza and mac-adjacent dishes, and I always end up with leftover pepperoni! I mean, great, but pepperoni is kind of specific, you know? So, I was making mac & cheese once and using bone broth (which makes this secretly protein- and nutrient-packed), and I just ended up throwing in the pepperoni. And the kids loved it! This recipe is so easy and fast, it takes nearly as little time and effort as the boxed kind.

- 1 tablespoon extra-virgin olive oil
- 1 small yellow onion, diced
- 5 ounces sliced mini pepperoni or regular pepperoni, chopped
- 2½ cups chicken stock or bone broth
- ¾ cup marinara sauce
- 1 teaspoon garlic powder
- ½ teaspoon Italian seasoning
- Kosher salt and freshly ground black pepper
- 2 cups small shell or elbow pasta
- ½ cup grated Parmesan cheese
- ½ cup shredded mozzarella cheese
- Chopped fresh basil leaves, for serving

In a large skillet over medium-high heat, heat the **oil**. Add the **onion** and cook, stirring frequently, until soft and translucent, about 3 minutes. Add the **pepperoni** and cook until slightly crispy, about 2 minutes. Stir in the **stock**, **marinara**, **garlic powder**, **Italian seasoning**, and **salt** and **pepper** to taste and bring to a boil. Add the **pasta**, reduce the heat to medium-low, and cover the skillet. Cook, stirring occasionally, until the pasta is tender but there is still a bit of liquid in the pan, 10 to 12 minutes. Remove the pan from the heat. Add the **Parmesan** and **mozzarella** and stir until completely melted.

Top with fresh **basil** and serve.

WAYS TO SERVE

- Better than Fresh, Frozen Broccoli in the Oven *(page 221)*
- Caesar Salad *(page 60)*
- Evergreen Lemony Parmesan Kale Salad *(page 59)*

Quick, Delish & Secretly Protein-Packed Creamy Marinara Pasta

FREEZER-FRIENDLY

SERVES 4 TO 6

Gluten-free friendly
Nut free

Kids (okay, and adults) can be tough eaters, and sometimes it can be a challenge to get enough protein in. A while back, I had some leftover cottage cheese, so I snuck it into some pasta sauce and all of my kids loved it! It adds such richness and creaminess without having to add heavy cream, and between the cottage cheese and the bone broth, there's enough protein that you don't need to add meat. Peas are another safe food for my kids, but if yours aren't into them, skip 'em! This sauce freezes really well, so it's another great recipe to make on its own (just skip the pasta) and freeze for another time.

- Kosher salt and freshly ground black pepper
- 8 ounces short pasta, such as penne, farfalle, or elbows
- 1 cup frozen peas
- 1 tablespoon extra-virgin olive oil
- 3 garlic cloves, minced
- 1 teaspoon Italian seasoning
- 1 (15-ounce) can diced tomatoes
- Juice of ½ lemon
- ½ cup cottage cheese
- ½ cup chicken stock or bone broth
- Grated Parmesan cheese, for serving
- Chopped fresh basil leaves, for serving

In a large pot of well-salted boiling water, cook the **pasta** according to the package instructions, adding the **peas** in the final 5 minutes of cooking. Reserve 1 cup of the pasta cooking water, remove the pot from the heat, and drain the pasta and peas. Set aside.

In a Dutch oven or large saucepan over medium heat, heat the **oil**. Add the **garlic** and **Italian seasoning** and cook, stirring frequently, until fragrant, 1 minute. Add the **tomatoes** and **lemon juice** and cook, stirring occasionally, until the mixture is thickened slightly, about 10 minutes. Remove the pot from the heat.

In a blender, carefully add the tomato mixture, plus the **cottage cheese**, **stock**, and **salt** and **pepper** to taste. Blend until completely smooth, thinning out the sauce if desired with a bit of stock or the reserved pasta water. (You can also do this with an immersion blender.)

Return the sauce to the pot, add the cooked pasta and peas, and toss well to combine. Add a bit more pasta water if needed to thin the sauce.

Top with **Parmesan** and fresh **basil** and serve.

WAYS TO SERVE

- Better than Fresh, Frozen Broccoli in the Oven *(page 221)*
- Caesar Salad *(page 60)*
- Evergreen Lemony Parmesan Kale Salad *(page 59)*

One-Skillet Creamy White Lasagna *with Chicken*

SERVES 4 TO 6

Gluten-free friendly
Nut free

So once upon a time, my oldest randomly boycotted anything with tomato sauce in it, or anything red. Which was, uh, unfortunate because I use it . . . all the time. So I had to get creative to make a cozy, easy meal for my kids without red sauce. The verdict: He loved it! And random toddler food boycotts aside, sometimes you want something creamy-dreamy instead of tomato-y. I always love to add basil at the end, but parsley or chives are great too.

2 boneless, skinless chicken breasts

Kosher salt and freshly ground black pepper

2 tablespoons extra-virgin olive oil

1 small yellow onion, chopped

3 garlic cloves, minced

1½ teaspoons Italian seasoning

1½ cups chicken stock or bone broth, plus more as needed

1 (13.5-ounce) can full-fat coconut milk

10 no-boil lasagna noodles (9 ounces), roughly broken into 1-inch pieces

3 cups packed baby spinach, roughly chopped

2 tablespoons chopped fresh parsley leaves

1 cup shredded mozzarella cheese

Place the **chicken breasts** on a cutting board or plate and season generously on both sides with **salt** and **pepper**.

In a large, high-sided, oven-safe skillet over medium-high heat, heat 1 tablespoon of the **oil**. Sear the chicken on both sides until deeply golden brown, 3 to 5 minutes per side. Remove the pan from the heat and transfer the chicken to a plate.

Return the skillet to medium-high heat and heat the remaining tablespoon of olive oil. Add the **onion** and season with salt and pepper. Cook, stirring frequently, until translucent, about 5 minutes. Add the **garlic** and **Italian seasoning** and cook until just fragrant, about 1 minute. Return the chicken breasts to the skillet and add the **stock**, stirring to loosen up any browned bits on the bottom of the skillet. Bring to a boil, reduce the heat to medium-low, and cover the skillet. Simmer until the chicken is cooked all the way through and measures 165°F, 10 to 15 minutes. Remove the pan from the heat. Transfer the chicken breasts to a cutting board and let rest for at least 5 minutes. Use forks or your hands to shred the chicken and set aside.

Return the pan to medium-high heat and add the **coconut milk** and broken **lasagna noodles**, stirring to coat the lasagna. Bring the mixture to a simmer and reduce the heat to medium. Cover and cook until the noodles are just tender, 10 to 15 minutes, stirring occasionally and adding more stock if needed. Add the **spinach**, **parsley**, and shredded chicken and stir well to combine. Cook until the spinach wilts and the chicken is warmed through, 3 to 5 minutes. Remove the pan from the heat.

Set the broiler to high heat.

Top the lasagna with the **mozzarella** and broil until the cheese is melted and bubbly, about 3 minutes. Serve hot.

Not-So-Boring Roasted Vegetable Pasta

SERVES 4 TO 6

Gluten-free friendly
Nut free

I am seriously so excited for you to try this roasted vegetable pasta. And okay, I never thought those words would come out my mouth, since it doesn't seem that most people get super excited about veggies. But! This pasta recipe will change your mind, I promise. Roasting the vegetables all together creates such a great depth of flavor, and the burst of tomatoes and artichokes really just takes it to another level. And the touch of cream cheese (gives me the tingles!) makes the sauce just creamy enough. If you or your kids are pickier about "seeing veggies," then absolutely puree the sauce—I usually do—but you can also serve as-is.

- 1½ cups cherry tomatoes
- 1 cup canned artichoke hearts, drained and chopped
- 1 medium red bell pepper, chopped
- 1 medium yellow onion, diced
- 1 medium zucchini, chopped
- 1 tablespoon tomato paste
- Extra-virgin olive oil
- Kosher salt and freshly ground black pepper
- 1 garlic head, halved widthwise through the middle
- 1 (12-ounce) package Italian chicken or pork sausage, sliced into ½-inch pieces (optional)
- 3 cups pasta, such as penne or farfalle
- 1 cup packed baby spinach
- ¼ cup plain cream cheese
- 3 tablespoons chopped fresh basil leaves, plus more for serving
- Grated Parmesan cheese, for serving

Preheat the oven to 400°F.

In a 9x13-inch casserole dish, add the **tomatoes**, **artichokes**, **bell pepper**, **onion**, **zucchini**, and **tomato paste**. Drizzle generously with **oil**, season well with **salt** and **pepper**, and toss to coat. Nestle the two halves of the **garlic** head into the vegetables and top it with a bit of oil and a sprinkle of salt. Roast for 30 minutes, undisturbed.

Stir the vegetables, being careful not to break up the garlic heads too much. Add the **chicken sausage** (if using) and toss to combine. Return the vegetables to the oven and roast until completely soft and slightly browned and caramelized along the edges, another 30 minutes.

In a large pot of well-salted boiling water, cook the **pasta** according to the package instructions. Remove the pot from the heat, reserve 1 cup of the pasta water, and drain. Set aside.

When the garlic is cool enough to handle, squeeze the cloves out into the baking dish. Add the **spinach** and **cream cheese** and stir well, letting the spinach wilt and the cream cheese melt into the vegetables. Add the cooked pasta and a splash of the reserved pasta water to help loosen up the sauce, and toss well to combine, adding more pasta water as needed. Add the **basil** and toss once more.

Serve immediately, topped with **Parmesan** and more fresh basil, if desired.

PREP TIP

If the thought of chopping veggies is the opposite of your love language, get the viral veggie chopper I always talk about on Instagram! Or just put on a podcast or playlist and jam out for a few minutes. Or better yet, call a relative or friend!

The Best *(and My Dad's Favorite)* Lasagna

FREEZER-FRIENDLY

SERVES 6 TO 8

Gluten-free friendly
Nut free

Anyone else have a loved one who asks for lasagna in the heat of summer?! I can't be the only one. My dad is truly the greatest of all time, so when he requested I make lasagna for his birthday dinner in July when it was 95 degrees, I wasn't going to argue. There are four dinners that remind me of my dad: meatloaf, chicken potpie, a sausage sandwich, and his beloved lasagna. Now, making lasagna always sounds more daunting than it is. I'd say this is a solid 15 to 20 minutes of effort before the oven does its thing. And the best part is that this absolutely serves a crowd, so it's ready for any and all gatherings. But even if you've got a small family yet love an easy freezer meal, let this be your new go-to.

Nonstick cooking spray

1 tablespoon extra-virgin olive oil

½ medium yellow onion, chopped

½ cup peeled, chopped carrots

1 pound ground beef, or your desired ground meat

1 teaspoon kosher salt

Freshly ground black pepper

2 tablespoons Italian seasoning

1 tablespoon onion powder

1 tablespoon garlic powder

4 cups marinara sauce

1 (15-ounce) container whole-milk ricotta cheese (about 2 cups)

1 cup grated Parmesan cheese

12 ounces frozen chopped spinach, thawed, excess moisture squeezed out

9 ounces no-boil lasagna noodles

1 pound shredded mozzarella cheese

WAYS TO SERVE

- Caesar Salad *(page 60)*
- Evergreen Lemony Parmesan Kale Salad *(page 59)*

Preheat the oven to 425°F. Spray a 9x13-inch casserole dish with nonstick cooking spray and set aside.

In a large skillet over medium-high heat, heat the **oil**. Add the **onion** and **carrots** and cook, stirring frequently, until beginning to soften, about 5 minutes. Add the **ground beef**, **salt**, and **pepper** to taste, and cook, stirring, until the beef is cooked through and no pink remains, about 7 minutes. Drain any excess fat.

Add the **Italian seasoning**, **onion powder**, and **garlic powder** and cook until just fragrant, 1 minute. Add the **marinara** and cook, stirring occasionally, until the sauce is warmed through and the flavors have combined, about 5 minutes. Remove the pan from the heat and set aside.

In a medium bowl, add the **ricotta**, **Parmesan**, and **spinach** and mix well to combine.

In the prepared casserole dish, add about 1 cup of the meat sauce and spread it to evenly cover the bottom of the dish. Place four sheets of the **lasagna noodles** side by side (it's okay if they overlap slightly). Top the lasagna sheets with another cup of sauce. Dollop about half of the ricotta mixture evenly over the sauce, followed by about a quarter of the **shredded mozzarella**. Repeat for two more layers, topping the last layer of lasagna sheets with the remaining meat sauce, followed by the remaining mozzarella.

Spray a large piece of aluminum foil with cooking spray and tightly cover the baking dish. Bake until the lasagna is bubbling and the cheese is starting to melt, about 40 minutes. Remove the foil and bake until the top is browned and bubbly, about 20 more minutes.

Let the lasagna cool for 10 to 15 minutes before serving.

SHEET PA

N MEALS

WE ALL NEED IN OUR LIVES

Sheet Pan Honey Mustard Salmon Bites *with Sweet Potatoes & Broccoli*

SERVES 4 TO 6

Gluten-free friendly
Dairy free
Nut free

There are certain foods we all know go together, like peanut butter and jelly. But a pairing that needs to be more hyped is salmon and honey mustard! Do *not* sleep on this combo, especially the homemade honey mustard that takes like a minute to whip up. This is my personal go-to meal for something that's healthy, flavorful, and doesn't require too much energy. My kids call the salmon bites "salmon nuggets" and they love to dip them in more honey mustard!

SALMON

- 1½ pounds fresh salmon, skin and any pin-bones removed, cut into 1-inch cubes
- 1 tablespoon extra-virgin olive oil
- 1 teaspoon Dijon mustard
- 1 teaspoon honey
- 1 teaspoon ground paprika
- ½ teaspoon kosher salt
- ½ teaspoon freshly ground black pepper
- ½ teaspoon garlic powder

HONEY MUSTARD SAUCE

- 3 tablespoons whole-grain mustard
- 1 tablespoon honey
- 1 tablespoon extra-virgin olive oil
- 2 garlic cloves, minced
- ½ teaspoon smoked paprika
- ½ teaspoon freshly ground black pepper
- Lemon wedges, for serving

SWEET POTATOES AND BROCCOLI

- 1 large sweet potato, any variety, cut into ½-inch cubes
- 1 head of broccoli, cut into bite-sized florets
- 3 medium shallots, thinly sliced
- 2 tablespoons extra-virgin olive oil
- ½ teaspoon garlic powder
- Kosher salt and freshly ground black pepper

MARINATE THE SALMON: In a medium bowl, add the cubed **salmon**, **oil**, **Dijon**, **honey**, **paprika**, **salt**, **pepper**, and **garlic powder** and toss well to coat. Set aside to marinate while you roast the vegetables.

MAKE THE HONEY MUSTARD SAUCE: In a medium bowl, whisk together the **mustard**, **honey**, **oil**, **garlic**, **smoked paprika**, and **pepper** until smooth. Set aside.

MAKE THE SWEET POTATOES AND BROCCOLI: Preheat the oven to 400°F. Line a baking sheet with parchment paper and set aside.

In a large bowl, add the **sweet potatoes**, **broccoli**, **shallots**, **oil**, **garlic powder**, and **salt** and **pepper** to taste and toss well to coat. Spread the vegetables in an even layer on the prepared baking sheet. Roast until some of the edges are beginning to brown, about 20 minutes. Flip the vegetables and continue roasting until the sweet potatoes are tender, another 10 to 15 minutes. Transfer the vegetables to a serving plate and set aside.

Add the marinated salmon cubes to the baking sheet in an even layer. Roast until the salmon is cooked through, 10 to 12 minutes. If you like, you can set the pan under the broiler for the last minute or two. Transfer the salmon to the plate with the vegetables.

Drizzle the honey mustard sauce over the salmon and vegetables and serve with **lemon wedges** on the side.

Our Go-To Nacho Night Nachos

SERVES 6

Gluten-free friendly
Nut free

My parents live in Florida for the majority of the year, and while it pains my soul not to have them near me, it does give us a great place to visit during the winter. When we're down there, if we don't know what to make for dinner or no one wants to put much effort into a meal, we make these nachos. Seriously, no one complains about eating tortilla chips, cheese, and all the nacho toppings! I'll typically use my Best Taco Meat recipe (page 114), which is truly my family's favorite, but you can customize with whatever meat you like, or keep it vegetarian. Either way, this is a lifesaver recipe. Keep it on hand for an easy game-day recipe too!

NACHOS

8 ounces salted tortilla chips

2 cups Best Taco Meat (page 114), Chipotle-Style Chicken (page 64), or any other cooked, seasoned meat

1 (15-ounce) can no-salt-added black beans, rinsed and drained

1 cup frozen corn

1 cup shredded cheddar cheese

½ cup shredded Manchego cheese

FOR SERVING

Diced Roma tomatoes

Super-Quick Guacamole (page 64), or diced avocado

Jarred chunky salsa (I use mild since the kids eat this)

Plain Greek yogurt (we love to use this just like sour cream), or sour cream

Chopped fresh cilantro leaves

Lime wedges

MAKE THE NACHOS: Preheat the oven to 400°F. Line a baking sheet with parchment paper.

Add the **tortilla chips** in a single layer to the prepared baking sheet. Evenly scatter the **meat**, **black beans**, **corn**, **cheddar**, and **Manchego** over the chips.

Bake until the cheeses have melted and are bubbly, 7 to 8 minutes. (If you want a little char on the nachos, place the pan under the broiler for the last few minutes, watching carefully so they don't burn.)

SERVE: Top as desired with **diced tomatoes**, **guacamole**, **salsa**, **yogurt**, and **cilantro**, with the **lime wedges** on the side for squeezing.

Sheet Pan Philly Cheesesteaks *with Homemade Cheesy Sauce*

SERVES 6

Gluten-free friendly
Nut free

My husband and I met in college about 20 minutes from Philadelphia, so as you can imagine, it was super common to go on a late-night Philly cheesesteak run. My kids love any cheesy sandwich, so I tinkered around with a recipe and they became obsessed with these. This is a great family meal that feels like a classic and a treat, but with a healthier twist. The cheese sauce in this truly won me over. It's way easier than you'd think!

STEAK AND PEPPERS

¼ cup extra-virgin olive oil

¼ cup coconut aminos

1 tablespoon Dijon mustard

1 teaspoon kosher salt

½ teaspoon garlic powder

½ teaspoon onion powder

¼ teaspoon freshly ground black pepper

1½ pounds sirloin steak, very thinly sliced

1 large yellow onion

1 medium green bell pepper

1 medium red bell pepper

8 ounces cremini mushrooms

6 long rolls, such as French or hoagie rolls

CHEESE SAUCE

2 tablespoons unsalted butter

1 tablespoon almond flour

½ cup milk of choice (dairy or nondairy), room temperature, plus more as needed

1 teaspoon Dijon mustard

1 teaspoon coconut aminos

¼ teaspoon garlic powder

¼ teaspoon onion powder

4 ounces provolone cheese, roughly chopped

Kosher salt

MAKE THE STEAK AND PEPPERS: Preheat the oven to 425°F. Line a baking sheet with parchment paper and set aside.

In a large bowl, whisk together the **oil**, **coconut aminos**, **Dijon**, **salt**, **garlic powder**, **onion powder**, and **pepper**. Add the **sliced steak**, toss well to coat, and let marinate while you prep the vegetables.

Thinly slice the **onion**, **green bell pepper**, **red bell pepper**, and **mushrooms**. As you finish prepping each, add it to the marinade and toss to coat. Spread out the mixture on the prepared baking sheet and roast until the steak is cooked through and the vegetables are softened, about 15 minutes.

MAKE THE CHEESE SAUCE: In a medium skillet over medium heat, melt the **butter**. Add the **almond flour** and cook, whisking constantly, to form a thick paste, about 1 minute. Whisk in the **milk**, followed by the **Dijon**, **coconut aminos**, **garlic powder**, and **onion powder**. Add the **cheese** and reduce the heat to low. Continue whisking until the cheese is completely melted and the sauce is smooth, about 5 minutes. If your sauce looks a bit thick, whisk in a bit more milk. Taste and check for seasoning, adding **salt** if needed. Remove the pan from the heat, cover to keep warm, and set aside.

Assemble the sandwiches: Preheat the broiler on high heat. Set a rack in the middle of the oven.

Open the **rolls** and toast them on the rack until golden, about 2 minutes. Divide the steak and vegetables between the rolls, drizzle the cheese sauce on top, and serve.

Weeknight Sheet Pan Chicken Parmesan *with Blistered Tomatoes*

SERVES 4 TO 6

Gluten-free friendly
Nut free

So you're craving chicken Parm, huh? Same with my husband, who wants this basically every week. The only problem is, I don't love the mess that frying chicken cutlets leaves all over my stovetop. To get around that, I found myself making a sheet pan version again and again, and now it's become our regular chicken Parm! The "breading" is almond flour or breadcrumbs and grated Parmesan (same as the Parmesan-Crusted Chicken Nuggets, page 102), so it's a tried-and-true approach. For serving, I usually keep things simple with pasta and jarred sauce on the side, and some sort of baby arugula dressed with lemon, olive oil, and yeah, more Parm.

3 cups grape or cherry tomatoes, left whole (so they blister a bit in the oven)

3 tablespoons extra-virgin olive oil

3 garlic cloves, minced

½ teaspoon dried oregano

¼ teaspoon crushed red pepper flakes (optional)

Kosher salt and freshly ground black pepper

2 large eggs

2 cups panko breadcrumbs, DIY Breadcrumbs (page 223), or almond flour

⅔ cup grated Parmesan cheese, plus more for serving

½ teaspoon garlic powder

1½ pounds boneless, skinless chicken breasts, cut in half lengthwise and pounded thin

Avocado oil spray

8 ounces fresh mozzarella cheese, thinly sliced

¼ cup fresh basil leaves, torn or roughly chopped

Preheat the oven to 450°F. Line a baking sheet with parchment paper and set aside.

In a medium bowl, toss together the **tomatoes**, 1 tablespoon of the **olive oil**, the **garlic**, **oregano**, **red pepper flakes** (if using), and **salt** and **pepper** to taste. Set aside.

In a wide, shallow bowl, add the **eggs** and beat lightly. In another wide, shallow bowl, use a fork to combine the **breadcrumbs**, **Parmesan**, **garlic powder**, and a pinch of salt.

Season the **chicken** generously with salt and pepper. Using a fork or your hands, dip each chicken breast in the eggs, followed by the breadcrumb mixture. Press the crumbs into the chicken and make sure the breasts are well covered, shaking off any excess. Lay the coated chicken breasts on the prepared baking sheet and spray the tops lightly with **avocado oil** (this will help it crisp more in the oven).

Bake until the breadcrumbs are starting to turn golden, about 8 minutes. Flip the chicken breasts and spoon the tomato mixture all around and between them. Return the pan to the oven and bake until the tomatoes have burst and the chicken is golden brown, another 10 minutes. Top the chicken with the **mozzarella**, return to the oven, and bake until the cheese is melted and the chicken has reached an internal temperature of 165°F, another 5 minutes or so. (You can also do this last part under the broiler if you prefer a more browned and bubbly top on the cheese! Just watch the pan carefully.)

Sprinkle the fresh **basil** on top of the chicken, and serve immediately with desired sides like a salad, veggies, or pasta.

Sheet Pan Basil Cashew Chicken

SERVES 4 TO 6

Gluten-free friendly
Nut free

My mom basically insisted I put this recipe in the book; it's her favorite! And honestly, I don't blame her. It definitely has that sticky-sweet-tangy sauce that we love in a takeout dish, but it's so much simpler than you might think. The real hack here is that it's a sheet pan meal, which makes it accessible even if you don't have a wok (and it means it's mostly hands-off during the cooking time!). And while the sauce has a ton of flavor, it's not spicy unless you add your own heat, so it's a real crowd-pleaser. It's really one of those dishes we make a few times a month, and I'm not someone who repeats a lot of recipes in my house!

SAUCE

¼ cup plus 2 tablespoons coconut aminos

2 tablespoons honey

2 tablespoons arrowroot or tapioca flour

2 garlic cloves, minced

1 tablespoon apple cider vinegar

1 teaspoon sesame oil

½ teaspoon fresh grated ginger, or ¼ teaspoon ground ginger

CHICKEN AND VEGETABLES

1 pound boneless, skinless chicken breasts or thighs, cut into 1-inch cubes

Kosher salt and freshly ground black pepper

1½ cups broccoli florets, fresh or frozen and thawed, larger florets cut in half

1 medium red bell pepper, cut into 1-inch pieces

1 large carrot, peeled and sliced into thin rounds

⅔ cup roasted unsalted cashews

1 tablespoon avocado oil

½ teaspoon garlic powder

My Tried & True Rice (page 213), Fluffy Quinoa (page 210), or any cooked grain, for serving

Chopped fresh basil leaves, for serving

Sesame seeds, for serving

MAKE THE SAUCE: In a medium saucepan over medium heat, add the **coconut aminos**, **honey**, **arrowroot flour**, **garlic**, **vinegar**, **sesame oil**, and **ginger**, plus ½ **cup water**, and whisk to combine. Bring to a simmer and cook, stirring frequently, until the sauce thickens, 3 to 5 minutes. Remove the pan from the heat and cover to keep warm.

MAKE THE CHICKEN AND VEGETABLES: Preheat the oven to 400°F. Line a baking sheet with parchment paper and set aside.

In a large bowl, season the **chicken** generously with **salt** and **pepper** and toss to coat. Add about 2 tablespoons of the sauce and toss well to coat. Add the chicken to the prepared baking sheet and bake for 8 minutes.

In the same large bowl, add the **broccoli**, **bell pepper**, **carrot**, **cashews**, and **avocado oil**, and toss to coat. Add the **garlic powder**, plus salt and pepper to taste, and toss again. Add the vegetables to the baking sheet in an even layer with the chicken and drizzle a few more tablespoons of the sauce over the vegetables. Bake until the vegetables are softened but still crisp and the chicken is cooked to 165°F, 8 to 12 minutes.

Transfer the chicken and vegetables to a serving bowl and drizzle with the remaining sauce. Serve over **rice** or **quinoa** with plenty of **basil** and **sesame seeds** on top.

Foolproof Sheet Pan Sausage & Gnocchi

SERVES 4 TO 6

Gluten-free friendly
Nut free

We used to live about five minutes from a Trader Joe's, so this became a staple recipe because I could buy all of the elements at one store! Obviously, you can get these ingredients almost anywhere now. The gnocchi get crispy here, and there's something about the flavor of sausage and gnocchi together—hearty and comforting. You can even do a tricolor situation here and drizzle some Ride-or-Die Kale Pesto (page 221) over the top. And one of the best parts? You don't have to clean up the stove or any mixing bowls after—it's truly a single pan!

Nonstick cooking spray

1 pound frozen potato or cauliflower gnocchi

5 mild Italian chicken sausage links, sliced into ½-inch pieces

1 medium red bell pepper, sliced

½ cup frozen peas

1½ cups marinara sauce

8 ounces fresh mozzarella cheese, torn or shredded

Chopped fresh basil leaves, for serving

Grated Parmesan cheese, for serving

Red pepper flakes, for serving (optional)

Preheat the oven to 425°F. Spray a baking sheet with **nonstick spray**.

Add the **gnocchi**, **sliced sausage**, **bell pepper**, and **peas** to the baking sheet in an even layer. (Separate any gnocchi that might be stuck together.) Pour the **marinara** on top and toss well to coat. Bake for 10 minutes and toss the mixture to help it cook evenly. Return the pan to the oven and continue baking until the gnocchi and pepper are tender, another 10 minutes or so. Top with the **mozzarella**, return the pan to the oven, and bake until the cheese is melted, about 5 minutes.

Serve hot, topped with the **basil**, **Parmesan**, and **red pepper flakes** (if using).

WAYS TO SERVE

- Caesar Salad *(page 60)*
- Evergreen Lemony Parmesan Kale Salad *(page 59)*
- Better than Fresh, Frozen Broccoli in the Oven *(page 221)*

SAFE SWAP

Don't love sausage? Sub a meat-free protein sausage, or crumbled veggie burgers!

Mini Broccoli Cheddar Meatloaves *with Roasted Veggies*

SERVES 4

Gluten free

I mean, are these not the cutest meatloaves ever?!! Why is everything even better in mini form? Maybe that's just me. The broccoli and cheddar flavors really come through and make these a little more special than a traditional meatloaf. Plus, they're a great handheld food for little ones. In homage to my dad, I serve them up with some potatoes and green beans, his favorite sides. One of my favorite things to do is make the meatloaves on their own, let them cool, and freeze them so I can take them out individually for busy nights when maybe not everyone is eating at the same time.

ROASTED VEGGIES

1 pound red or yellow baby potatoes, washed and halved

2 cups fresh green beans, ends trimmed

1 tablespoon extra-virgin olive oil

½ teaspoon garlic powder

Kosher salt and freshly ground black pepper

MEATLOAVES

1 pound ground beef

1 cup chopped broccoli florets, fresh or frozen and thawed

½ cup shredded cheddar cheese

¼ cup almond flour

1 large egg

2 scallions, thinly sliced (white and green parts)

1 teaspoon kosher salt

½ teaspoon dried basil

Freshly ground black pepper

2 tablespoons DIY Ketchup (page 225) or regular ketchup, plus more for serving

1½ tablespoons extra-virgin olive oil

MAKE THE VEGGIES: Preheat the oven to 425°F. Line a baking sheet with parchment paper and set aside.

In a large bowl, add the **potatoes**, **green beans**, **oil**, **garlic powder**, and **salt** and **pepper** to taste. Toss well to coat and spread out the mixture on the prepared baking sheet. Roast the vegetables while you mix up the meatloaf, about 10 minutes.

MAKE THE MEATLOAVES: Set a wire rack over a baking sheet and set aside.

In a medium bowl, add the **ground beef**, **broccoli**, **cheddar**, **almond flour**, **egg**, **scallions**, **salt**, **basil**, and **pepper** to taste. Mix until incorporated, using your hands (I like to use food-handling gloves here). Shape the meat mixture into 4 small loaves, about 4x3 inches each. Set the mini meatloaves on the prepared rack.

In a small bowl, whisk together the **ketchup** and **oil** and brush the mixture all over the meatloaves.

Remove the baking sheet with the vegetables from the oven and give the pan a shake to help the vegetables flip and brown evenly. Return the vegetables to the oven, along with the meatloaves. Bake until the center of each meatloaf reaches 165°F and the vegetables are tender and golden, 30 to 35 minutes.

Serve hot with additional ketchup or any other desired condiments.

Twice-Baked Cheesy Pesto Spaghetti Squash

SERVES 4

Gluten free
Nut free

I know spaghetti squash can be kind of divisive—I love it and have been eating it for years, but for a long time, I couldn't get my kids to eat it. Then I made this dish (which, let's be real, I made for me) and they liked it! What did I do to get them to eat this? I mean, it's topped with melted, bubbly cheese, so I think that drew them in. If spaghetti squash kind of mystifies you, too, this is a great gateway recipe because you're just roasting the squash, mixing some other stuff in, and plonking it all right back in the squash. I love sausage or rotisserie chicken here, but you can leave it vegetarian or add any other protein you like.

- 2 medium spaghetti squash
- 2 cups shredded mozzarella cheese
- 1 cup grated Parmesan cheese, plus more for serving
- 1 cup cooked crumbled Italian sausage, ground beef, or ground chicken (optional)
- ¼ cup Ride-or-Die Kale Pesto (page 221), or any store-bought pesto
- 3 tablespoons extra-virgin olive oil
- 2 garlic cloves, minced
- 2 teaspoons dried basil
- 1 teaspoon dried oregano
- Kosher salt and freshly ground black pepper

Preheat the oven to 425°F. Line a baking sheet with parchment paper and set aside.

Using a sharp knife, carefully cut the **squash** in half lengthwise. Scoop out and discard the seeds. Place the squash halves cut side down on the prepared baking sheet. Roast until very tender, about 45 minutes.

In a medium bowl, combine ½ cup of the **mozzarella**, the **Parmesan**, crumbled **sausage** (if using), **pesto**, **oil**, **garlic**, **basil**, **oregano**, and **salt** and **pepper** to taste. Set aside.

Using a large spoon, carefully scoop out about 90 percent of the cooked squash from each half and add it to the bowl with the pesto-and-cheese mixture. Mix well to combine. Divide the mixture between the hollowed-out squash halves on the baking sheet and top with the remaining mozzarella.

Return the squash to the oven and bake until the cheese is melted and bubbly, another 8 to 10 minutes.

Top with additional Parmesan, if desired, and serve hot.

THE DESSERT

STASH

Go-To, Crowd-Pleaser Key Lime Pie *with Graham Cracker Crust*

MAKES 1 (9-INCH) PIE

Gluten free
Nut free

Another birthday request from my dad! (But at least this felt weather-appropriate for a hot July night.) He loves a dessert more than anyone I know, and growing up we used to go to the Keys in Florida, so we ate our fair share of key lime pie. This is my version of the classic, and I'm so proud of how it came out. The pie crust itself is foolproof to make (truly, you can do it!), but if you find yourself in a pinch, you can 100 percent use store-bought pie crust. I tend to lean more into my coconut whipped cream to serve with this, but it will work beautifully with any whipped cream, dairy or not, store-bought or homemade. I have made this dozens of times and it never fails. The key is serving it well-chilled!

PREP TIP

Don't want to make your own whipped cream? No problem! Store-bought is an option for a reason!

GRAHAM CRACKER CRUST

Avocado oil spray, for the pan

About 21 square graham crackers, gluten-free if needed

5 tablespoons unsalted butter, melted

¼ cup coconut sugar

½ teaspoon ground cinnamon

¼ teaspoon freshly grated or ground nutmeg

¼ teaspoon kosher salt

KEY LIME FILLING

4 large egg yolks

1¾ cups sweetened condensed coconut milk

½ cup bottled key lime juice or freshly squeezed lime juice

Grated zest of 1 lime, plus more for serving

COCONUT WHIPPED CREAM

1 (14-ounce) can full-fat coconut milk or coconut cream, chilled in the fridge overnight

2 tablespoons powdered sugar, sifted, plus more as needed

½ teaspoon vanilla extract

recipe continues

MAKE THE CRUST: Preheat the oven to 350°F. Spray a 9-inch pie dish with **avocado oil** and set aside.

In a food processor, add the **graham crackers** and pulse into fine crumbs. This should yield about 1½ cups of crumbs. Transfer the crumbs to a medium bowl and add the **melted butter**, **coconut sugar**, **cinnamon**, **nutmeg**, and **salt**, and use a silicone spatula to combine.

Add the mixture to the prepared pie dish. Use the spatula or the bottom of a glass to flatten the mixture at the base of the dish and work the mixture evenly up around the sides. Bake until fragrant and slightly golden, about 10 minutes. Set aside to cool completely before adding the filling (*completely,* or the filling won't set).

MAKE THE FILLING: Preheat the oven to 375°F.

In a medium bowl, add the **egg yolks** and whisk vigorously until fluffy and slightly lighter in color, about 1 minute. Add the **sweetened condensed coconut milk**, **lime juice**, and **lime zest** and whisk until smooth and fully combined, another minute.

Pour the mixture into the cooled pie crust and bake until the filling is set, with a slight wobble, 15 to 20 minutes. Let the pie cool completely, then cover and chill for at least 4 hours.

MAKE THE COCONUT WHIPPED CREAM: Set a medium metal bowl and wire beaters in the freezer for at least 30 minutes. (This can be the bowl and whisk attachment from a stand mixer, or just a regular mixing bowl and beaters from a hand mixer.)

Open the can of **chilled coconut milk** and scoop all of the solidified cream from the top into the chilled bowl. Attach the chilled beaters or whisk to the mixer, and beat the coconut cream on medium speed until smooth and slightly fluffy, about 1 minute. Add the **powdered sugar** and **vanilla** and beat on low speed until incorporated. Taste and add more powdered sugar if you'd like it sweeter.

Cover and refrigerate for at least 2 hours and up to 3 days. It will thicken as it chills.

Dollop the coconut whipped cream onto the chilled pie, zest a bit of lime on top, and serve.

Yes, You Can Make a Cake from Scratch: Funfetti Sheet Cake *with Vanilla Buttercream Frosting*

MAKES 1 (12X17-INCH) CAKE

Gluten free
Nut free

Like a lot of moms, mine always used a boxed mix for our birthday cakes growing up. Were they always delicious and special? Yeah! But I since realized that it's often just as easy to make your own mix, and this one is a foolproof base for any flavors and add-ins that your family loves. For my kids, that's sprinkles, but you can add chocolate chips, or add a dash of cinnamon to the batter and frosting for a spice cake, or leave it all-vanilla and add coconut shavings on top. And speaking of the top: this buttercream is LEGIT, people. It's way easier and less intimidating than people think!

FUNFETTI CAKE

Nonstick cooking spray
1½ cups coconut sugar
4 large eggs
1 cup milk of choice (dairy or nondairy)
½ cup (1 stick) unsalted butter, melted and cooled slightly
⅓ cup plain Greek yogurt or coconut yogurt
¼ cup avocado oil or liquid coconut oil
1 tablespoon vanilla extract
½ teaspoon almond extract
3 cups all-purpose flour, gluten-free if needed
1 tablespoon baking powder
½ teaspoon kosher salt
½ cup rainbow sprinkles, plus more for topping

FROSTING

½ cup (1 stick) unsalted butter, softened
½ cup canned coconut cream, room temperature
4 cups powdered sugar
1 tablespoon vanilla extract

MAKE THE CAKE: Preheat the oven to 350°F. Grease a 12x17-inch jelly roll pan with cooking spray and set aside.

In a large bowl, whisk together the **coconut sugar**, **eggs**, **milk**, **butter**, **yogurt**, **avocado oil**, **vanilla**, and **almond extract** until smooth. Add the **flour**, **baking powder**, and **salt** and whisk again to combine. Using a silicone spatula, fold in the sprinkles.

Add the cake batter to the prepared pan and spread it in an even layer. Bake until a cake tester or toothpick comes out clean, about 30 minutes. If you find the cake is browning too quickly, cover with foil and continue baking.

Let the cake cool completely on a wire rack before frosting.

MAKE THE FROSTING: In the bowl of a stand mixer fitted with the paddle attachment, beat the **butter** on high speed until pale and fluffy, about 5 minutes. Add the **coconut cream** and beat on medium speed until incorporated, about 30 seconds. Add 1 cup of the **powdered sugar** and beat on medium speed until incorporated, less than a minute. Repeat with the remaining powdered sugar, adding it 1 cup at a time. Add the **vanilla** and mix on low speed until combined.

Frost the cooled cake with the buttercream, top with lots of sprinkles, and serve.

Crispy-Crunchy-Nutty Balls

FREEZER-FRIENDY

Makes about 20 (1½-inch) balls

Gluten free
Dairy free

I first made a version of these during the early days of the Covid pandemic, right around my thirtieth birthday. Back then, we lived in Hoboken and my parents lived just a couple miles away, so they'd come over all the time asking what I'd made lately as they poked around in my fridge and pantry. They became some of the original taste-testers for my recipes, and my mom especially loved these from the get-go. These are kind of reminiscent of a Butterfinger candy bar! At the time, I made them in more of a log format (to mimic the original candy bar), but I noticed wherever I brought them, people would want to split them, so I started making them in two-bite balls. Along the way I also added cornflakes, which I really think sends the crunch factor over the top!

1 cup creamy peanut or almond butter (as drippy as you can find!)

⅓ cup maple syrup or honey

¾ cup brown rice cereal

¾ cup cornflakes

1½ cups semisweet, dark, or milk chocolate chips

Sea salt, for sprinkling (optional)

In a small saucepan, add the **peanut butter** and **maple syrup**. Set over medium-low heat and let the mixture soften and melt, stirring frequently, until combined, just 1 or 2 minutes. Remove the pan from the heat.

In a medium bowl, add the peanut butter mixture, plus the **brown rice cereal** and **cornflakes**. Use a silicone spatula to fold the mixture together to combine. Set the bowl in the fridge for 15 minutes to firm up.

Line a baking sheet with parchment paper and set aside.

Using a tablespoon or a small cookie scoop, scoop out a portion of the peanut butter–cereal mixture and roll it into a 1½-inch ball. Add the ball to the prepared baking sheet and repeat with the remaining mixture. Place the baking sheet in the fridge to set for 10 to 15 minutes.

In a small saucepan, add the **chocolate**. Set the pan over low heat and melt the chocolate, stirring frequently. (You can also do this in 15-second intervals in the microwave.) Remove the pan from the heat.

Using a fork and spoon, dip each peanut butter ball into the melted chocolate, rolling it around gently to coat. Return the ball to the baking sheet and repeat with the remaining peanut butter balls and chocolate. Sprinkle the balls with **sea salt**, if using. Return the baking sheet to the fridge or freezer to let the chocolate harden completely.

Store in an airtight container in the refrigerator for up to 1 week, or in the freezer for up to 2 months.

SAFE SWAP

Allergic to nuts? Sub in tahini—it's another great option for these!

Peanut Butter Magic Cookie Bars

MAKES 9 BARS

Gluten free

FREEZER-FRIENDLY

When I was in college, I'd treat myself to these insanely good "magic cookie bars" from a local coffee shop. They were a version of what some people would call a seven-layer bar or a dream bar, depending on where you're from. So when I wanted to do my own twist on these bars, you know I had to do a peanut butter version, complete with a *peanut butter caramel!* Can you believe it? It's simply addictive and when it's combined with the chocolate chips, almonds, and coconut, you'll know why I call these magic. I love making them for a cookie exchange, so definitely flag these for all your holiday baking!

PEANUT BUTTER CARAMEL

- 1 (15.5-ounce) can full-fat coconut milk
- ½ cup coconut sugar
- ¼ cup creamy peanut butter (I use the super drippy stuff!)
- ½ teaspoon vanilla extract

BARS

- Nonstick cooking spray
- 1 cup almond flour
- 3 tablespoons creamy peanut butter
- 2 tablespoons maple syrup
- 2 tablespoons melted coconut oil
- ½ teaspoon ground cinnamon
- ¾ cup dark chocolate chips
- ½ cup coarsely chopped peanuts
- ¼ cup coarsely chopped almonds
- ¼ cup unsweetened coconut flakes

MAKE THE CARAMEL: In a medium saucepan over medium heat, add the **coconut milk** and **coconut sugar**. Cook, stirring often, until the mixture comes to a boil, about 10 minutes. Reduce the heat to medium-low and continue cooking, stirring occasionally, until the sauce reaches a thick, caramel consistency, 25 to 30 minutes. Remove the pan from the heat. Add the **peanut butter** and **vanilla**, stir until completely smooth, and set aside.

MAKE THE BARS: Preheat the oven to 350°F. Line an 8x8-inch metal baking pan with parchment paper, grease lightly with **nonstick spray**, and set aside. (You can use a glass dish if that's what you have, just note that the bars will take longer to bake.)

In a large bowl, add the **almond flour**, **peanut butter**, **maple syrup**, **coconut oil**, and **cinnamon**. Use a silicone spatula to combine, mixing until uniform. Transfer the mixture into the prepared baking dish and press it into an even layer. Scatter the **chocolate chips**, **peanuts**, **almonds**, and **coconut flakes** over the crust layer, and evenly pour the caramel sauce on top.

Bake until the crust is set and the chocolate chips are melted, about 25 minutes. Let cool completely on a wire rack, chill in the fridge for at least 1 hour, and cut into squares.

Store the bars in an airtight container in the fridge for up to 1 week, or in the freezer for up to 2 months.

Foolproof 4-Ingredient Copycat Orange-Vanilla Pops

FREEZER-FRIENDLY

MAKES 6 POPS (DEPENDING ON YOUR MOLDS)

Gluten free
Dairy-free friendly
Nut free

One summer, my son came home from camp yelling, "MOM! I HAD AN ORANGE! ICE CREAM! POPSICLE!" And in that moment, I realized he'd discovered Creamsicles. And why are they weirdly hard to find in the store nowadays? I love that my kids are getting into them now (I loved them as a kid, too), and this four-ingredient situation means I don't have to search high and low for them in the store. If you've been following me for a while, you know I do a lot of Popsicle-adjacent stuff, but I'd never done an orange-vanilla flavor, so it was time for this to join the family. And dare I say, I think these are the new favorite!

- 2 medium oranges, peeled (about 1½ cups of fruit)
- 1¼ cups plain Greek yogurt or coconut yogurt
- 2 tablespoons maple syrup or honey
- ½ teaspoon vanilla extract

In a blender, add the **oranges**, **yogurt**, **maple syrup**, and **vanilla** and blend until completely smooth. Divide the mixture into ice pop molds and freeze until very firm (I like to let them set overnight).

To serve, run each ice pop mold under warm running water to help loosen the pop.

The Perfect Gluten-Free Chocolate Chip Cookies

FREEZER-FRIENDLY

MAKES ABOUT 2 DOZEN COOKIES

Gluten-free friendly
Dairy-free friendly

I think my mom burned herself out on baking when I was a kid, because she will be the first person to tell you she is *the* laziest baker nowadays. And yet, she makes these cookies all the time. In fact, I think they're the only thing she will still bake from scratch. She always keeps these in the freezer—such a great move, because have you ever had a frozen cookie?? INCREDIBLE. If you don't do gluten-free, you'll still love them, but if you do, these will change your life. They turn out perfect every time.

1 cup coconut sugar

½ cup (1 stick) unsalted butter, melted and slightly cooled, or liquid coconut oil

1 large egg

½ teaspoon vanilla extract

1¼ cups almond flour

1 cup all-purpose flour, gluten-free if needed

1 teaspoon baking powder

¼ teaspoon kosher salt

½ cup semisweet or dark chocolate chips

⅓ cup chopped walnuts (optional)

Flaky salt (optional)

Preheat the oven to 350°F. Line a baking sheet with parchment paper and set aside.

In a large bowl, whisk together the **coconut sugar**, **butter**, **egg**, and **vanilla** until smooth. Add the **almond flour**, **all-purpose flour**, **baking powder**, and **kosher salt** and use a silicone spatula to combine. Fold in the **chocolate chips** and **walnuts** (if using).

Using a cookie scoop or spoon, scoop about 2 tablespoons of cookie dough and add it to the prepared baking sheet. (You can roll these in your hands to smooth them out, but keeping them rough makes some nice craggy areas for the flaky salt later.) Repeat with the remaining dough, leaving about ½ inch of space between cookies. These won't spread much! Sprinkle with **flaky salt** (if using) and bake until the cookies are just set, 10 to 12 minutes.

Let the cookies cool on the pan for at least 5 minutes before serving.

Store extra cookies in an airtight container in the fridge for up to 1 week, or in the freezer for up to 2 months.

Dreamy Peanut Butter Cup Pie

MAKES 1 (8- OR 9-INCH) PIE

Gluten free

Hands down, this is my favorite dessert recipe in the entire book! Birthdays, anniversaries, random dinner parties—this is what I'm making. If you've followed me for any amount of time, you know that peanut butter is my number one favorite food, followed closely by chocolate! Now, don't let the homemade crust intimidate you; this really does come together seamlessly. I love this as an alternative to more traditional pies during the winter holidays, and it's incredible at summer barbecues!

CRUST

Nonstick cooking spray

2¼ cups almond flour

⅓ cup cocoa powder

¼ teaspoon kosher salt

¼ cup avocado oil or liquid coconut oil

¼ cup maple syrup or honey

1 teaspoon vanilla extract

PEANUT BUTTER FILLING

¾ cup creamy peanut butter, room temperature (I use the super drippy stuff!)

8 ounces plain cream cheese or nondairy cream cheese, room temperature

¼ cup maple syrup or honey

1 (9-ounce) container frozen coconut whipped topping, thawed

TOPPINGS (OPTIONAL)

Crushed peanut butter cups

Chopped dark chocolate or mini semisweet chocolate chips

Coconut whipped topping

MAKE THE CRUST: Preheat the oven to 350°F. Grease an 8- or 9-inch pie dish with **nonstick spray** and set aside.

In a medium bowl, combine the **almond flour**, **cocoa powder**, and **salt**. Add the **avocado oil**, **maple syrup**, and **vanilla** and mix well until thoroughly combined. Tip out the mixture into the prepared pie dish and press it gently into a uniform crust, working it all the way up the sides as well. Bake until fragrant, about 20 minutes. Let cool completely before filling.

MAKE THE FILLING: In the bowl of a stand mixer fitted with the paddle attachment, add the **peanut butter** and **cream cheese** and beat on medium speed until fluffy and well combined, scraping the sides of the bowl with a spatula as needed, about 3 minutes. Add the **maple syrup** and beat on low speed until combined, about 1 minute. Add the **coconut whipped topping** and beat until combined, 1 or 2 minutes.

Add the filling to the cooled crust, smoothing the top with a silicone spatula. Cover and refrigerate until the filling is firmly set, at least 4 hours and up to overnight.

Decorate with desired toppings and serve chilled.

Mixed Berry Pie Crumb Bars

FREEZER-FRIENDLY

MAKES ABOUT 9 BARS

Gluten-free friendly
Dairy free
Nut free

If you know me, you know I'm normally more of a peanut butter and chocolate lover, but man, these bars made me realize I don't highlight berry desserts as much as I should! These have become the ultimate summer barbecue dessert in my life: my parents LOVE anything with berries, my good friend isn't much of a chocolate person, and these bars are light and fresh but still sweet enough that kids adore them. I use frozen berries for this because I kind of like how they get saucier than fresh berries, but if you've got fresh ones to use up, absolutely go for it. And at my house, the vanilla ice cream on top is required! (Dairy-free coconut ice cream is also amazing with this.)

CRUMBLE

- Nonstick cooking spray
- 1½ cups oat flour
- 1 cup old-fashioned or quick oats
- ½ cup coconut sugar
- ½ teaspoon ground cinnamon
- ¼ teaspoon baking soda
- ¼ teaspoon kosher salt
- ½ cup melted coconut oil
- 1 teaspoon vanilla extract
- Vanilla ice cream, for serving (optional)

FILLING

- 2½ cups frozen mixed berries (I do a mix of blueberries, raspberries, and strawberries)
- 3 tablespoons maple syrup
- Grated zest of 1 lemon
- ½ teaspoon vanilla extract
- Pinch of kosher salt
- 1 tablespoon tapioca or arrowroot flour

MAKE THE CRUMBLE: Preheat the oven to 350°F. Line an 8x8-inch metal baking pan with parchment paper and spray with **nonstick spray**. (You can use a glass dish if that's what you have, just note that the bars will take longer to bake.)

In a large bowl, add the **oat flour**, **oats**, **coconut sugar**, **cinnamon**, **baking soda**, and **salt**, using a fork to combine. Add the **coconut oil** and **vanilla** and mix until a crumbly texture forms. Add 1⅔ cups of the mixture into the prepared pan and use your hands to press it into an even layer. Place the remaining mixture in the fridge; you'll use it later for the topping.

MAKE THE FILLING: In a medium saucepan over medium heat, combine the **frozen fruit**, **maple syrup**, **lemon zest**, **vanilla**, and **salt**. As the fruit softens, use a wooden spoon to press and break down the berries a bit. Bring to a simmer, reduce the heat to low, and whisk in the **arrowroot flour**. Simmer, stirring occasionally, until the mixture is thickened and a little jammy, 3 to 5 minutes. Remove the pan from the heat.

Spread the fruit mixture evenly over the prepared crust and top with the reserved crumble mixture. Bake until the filling is bubbly and the top is slightly golden, about 30 minutes.

Let cool in the pan for 30 minutes. From here, you can slice into bars and serve warm or chill them in the fridge and enjoy cold. Either way, ice cream is highly recommended. You can even store these in the freezer for up to 2 months; just thaw in the fridge first before serving.

Crispy-Chewy Oatmeal Raisin Cookies

FREEZER-FRIENDLY

MAKES ABOUT 2 DOZEN COOKIES

Gluten-free friendly
Dairy free
Nut-free friendly

Where do I begin with these?? I feel like oatmeal raisin cookies are the forgotten child of cookies. Is it the slightly wholesome vibe they give off? I don't know, but whenever I have one I think, "Wait, why don't I eat these more often?" These are so simple and really take only minutes of effort. And, maybe the best part, you can bake them from frozen! Just portion the dough before chilling in the freezer and keep them there until you're ready to bake. (You can even stash the pre-portioned cookies in a freezer-safe container and bake on demand. The dream!) I love these as a breakfast cookie, and unlike a lot of gluten-free cookies, they have a texture that keeps well even after a few days.

- ½ cup plus 2 tablespoons coconut sugar
- ½ cup melted coconut oil
- 1 large egg
- 2 tablespoons maple syrup
- 1½ teaspoons vanilla extract
- 1½ cups old-fashioned or quick oats
- 1 cup oat flour
- 1 teaspoon baking powder
- ½ teaspoon ground cinnamon
- ¼ teaspoon kosher salt
- ¾ cup dark raisins
- ½ cup chocolate chips (optional)
- ⅓ cup walnuts (optional)

Preheat the oven to 350°F. Line a baking sheet with parchment paper and set aside.

In a large bowl, whisk together the **coconut sugar**, **coconut oil**, **egg**, **maple syrup**, and **vanilla**. Add the **oats**, **oat flour**, **baking powder**, **cinnamon**, and **salt** and use a silicone spatula to combine. Fold in the **raisins**, **chocolate chips** (if using), and **walnuts** (if using). Set the bowl in the freezer for 15 minutes, until the dough is firm (you can also chill the dough in the fridge for about 1 hour).

Using a cookie scoop or spoon, portion the dough into small balls and space them evenly apart on the prepared baking sheet. The cookies will spread, but not much, so you should be able to fit them on the same baking sheet. But if not, or you don't want to risk it, feel free to use a second sheet.

Smudge a small amount of coconut oil on the back of a spoon and flatten the cookies about halfway (the dough can be sticky, so the oil helps!). If you like a fluffier cookie, only press down a little. Bake until the cookies are fragrant and look mostly matte, 12 to 15 minutes. Set the baking sheet on a cooling rack and let the cookies cool for at least 10 minutes before serving.

Store in an airtight container at room temperature for up to 5 days, in the fridge for up to 2 weeks, or in the freezer for up to 2 months.

One-Bowl Extra-Extra Fudgy Brownie Loaf

FREEZER-FRIENDLY

MAKES 1 (9-INCH) LOAF

Gluten free
Dairy-free friendly
Nut free

This has been on my site for years and years, and it still hits after all this time. My friend says it's her family's all-time favorite snacky dessert. Honestly, it's a chocolate lover's dream: it's fudgy, it's moist, and it's a one-bowl, so as special as it tastes, it's also a really easy anytime treat. I like using dark chocolate for this; I think the bitterness makes it sophisticated and balances the sweetness in the cake. If you want to know the way to my heart, this is it! I'd literally make this for my own birthday.

Nonstick cooking spray

1 cup milk of choice (dairy or nondairy)

½ cup liquid coconut oil

1 large egg

1 teaspoon vanilla extract

2½ cups almond flour

¾ cup coconut sugar

½ cup cocoa powder

1 tablespoon baking powder

¼ teaspoon kosher salt

1 cup dark chocolate chips

Preheat the oven to 350°F. Line a 9-inch loaf pan with parchment paper, grease with **nonstick spray**, and set aside.

In a large bowl, whisk together the **milk**, **coconut oil**, **egg**, and **vanilla** until smooth. Add the **almond flour**, **coconut sugar**, **cocoa powder**, **baking powder**, and **salt** and whisk again until smooth. Fold in half of the **chocolate chips** with a silicone spatula. Transfer the batter to the prepared loaf pan and sprinkle the remaining chocolate chips on top.

Bake until a cake tester or toothpick comes out mostly clean, 1 hour to 1 hour and 15 minutes. This cake will be very moist in the middle, even when baked all the way (think lava cake vibes), so if you're more comfortable with a temperature reading, look for an internal reading of 200°F.

Let the cake cook on a wire rack for at least 15 minutes before slicing. Serve warm, room temperature, or chilled.

Simple, Yet Looks Fancy Strawberry Banana Pudding

SERVES 6 TO 8

Gluten-free friendly
Dairy-free friendly
Nut free

I stumbled into this recipe when I made it for my book club! I was playing around with a yogurt-based banana pudding recipe when I remembered how much I love any strawberry-banana combo. Sure enough, my friends devoured the whole thing (and this recipe makes a lot!). This is one of those desserts that you can take to a cookout or any gathering, and it looks so much fancier than it actually is to make. And of course, my kids love it. One tip: I'd say this is one of a handful of recipes in this book that isn't great to make ahead, only because the vanilla wafers can get a bit soggy. Luckily, it's easy enough to throw together before an event and can chill in the fridge for up to 2 hours.

4 cups plain or vanilla Greek yogurt or coconut yogurt

¼ cup coconut sugar

1 teaspoon vanilla extract

1 cup frozen or fresh, hulled strawberries

4 medium bananas, sliced, plus more for serving

2½ cups vanilla wafers, plus more for serving

Coconut whipped topping, for serving

Sliced fresh strawberries, for serving

In a medium bowl, whisk together the **yogurt**, **coconut sugar**, and **vanilla**. Set aside.

In a blender, add the **strawberries** and half of the yogurt mixture and blend until completely smooth (and pink!). Set aside.

Add half of the sliced **bananas** to the bowl with the vanilla yogurt mixture and fold to gently combine.

In an 8x8-inch baking dish or large glass bowl, spread one-quarter of the banana pudding on the bottom of the dish. Top with a layer of the **vanilla wafers**, followed by a layer of the sliced bananas, followed by one-quarter of the strawberry pudding. Repeat with the remaining ingredients; the total number of layers will vary depending on the size of your dish. Cover and chill for at least 2 hours, and no longer than 8 hours.

Serve topped with the **coconut whipped topping**, plus more vanilla wafers, **strawberries**, and sliced bananas.

Absolutely Epic Brownie Cookie Bars

MAKES 9 BARS

Gluten free

FREEZER-FRIENDLY

My friend owns an organizing business and a few years ago, she came to help us organize our playroom. To say thank you, I baked these for her. Now, I make food for her all the time, so she's had a lot of my cooking. But she said these were the best thing I'd ever made, and insisted they go in the book! I make these often as a sweet snack to have around the house, but they're also fun enough for a special occasion. An important tip: Use super drippy peanut butter! And if you're not a peanut butter person, I also really love tahini in this.

BROWNIE LAYER

- Nonstick cooking spray
- 1 cup creamy peanut butter (use the super drippy kind) or tahini
- ⅓ cup maple syrup
- ¼ cup coconut sugar
- 1 large egg
- 1 teaspoon vanilla extract
- ¼ cup cocoa powder
- ½ teaspoon baking powder
- ¼ teaspoon kosher salt

CHOCOLATE CHIP COOKIE LAYER

- ½ cup coconut sugar
- ⅓ cup avocado or melted coconut oil
- 1 large egg
- 1 teaspoon vanilla extract
- 2 cups almond flour
- 1 teaspoon baking soda
- ¼ teaspoon kosher salt
- ½ cup dark chocolate chips

MAKE THE BROWNIE LAYER: Preheat the oven to 350°F. Line an 8x8-inch metal baking pan with parchment paper, spray with **nonstick spray**, and set aside. (You can use a glass dish if that's what you have, just note that the bars will take longer to bake.)

In a large bowl, add the **peanut butter**, **maple syrup**, **coconut sugar**, **egg**, and **vanilla** and use a silicone spatula to combine thoroughly. Add the **cocoa powder**, **baking powder**, and **salt** and mix well into a thick batter. Add the batter to the prepared baking dish, spread it in an even layer, and set aside.

MAKE THE COOKIE LAYER: Wipe out the mixing bowl. Add the **coconut sugar**, **avocado oil**, **egg**, and **vanilla** and whisk until smooth. Add the **almond flour**, **baking soda**, and **salt** and mix with a silicone spatula. Fold in the **chocolate chips**.

Spread the cookie dough over the brownie batter in an even layer. Bake until the cookie layer is light golden brown, about 20 minutes. Cover the dish with foil and bake until a cake tester or toothpick comes out clean, 10 to 15 more minutes.

Place the baking dish on a rack to let cool completely. Slice into bars and serve.

Store extra bars in an airtight container in the fridge for up to 5 days, or in the freezer for up to 2 months.

My Mama's Ooey Gooey Apple Blondies

FREEZER-FRIENDLY

MAKES 9 BARS

Gluten-free friendly
Nut-free friendly

This dessert is absolutely iconic in my family and I'm thrilled to be sharing it in this book! When I was growing up, we went apple picking every single fall, usually around Rosh Hashanah because I was off school. My dad has a notorious sweet tooth and always needed to have a dessert in the house, so my mom would save some of the fresh apples to bake with and usually, she'd turn them into these cozy bars. When I met my husband over 15 years ago, he fell in love with them instantly. Now we take our own kids apple picking and it's such a sweet tradition. Of course, you don't have to wait for fall to make these, but no fall meal in my family is complete without them.

Nonstick cooking spray

½ cup (1 stick) unsalted butter, softened

2 cups coconut sugar

2 large eggs

1 teaspoon vanilla extract

1½ cups all-purpose flour, gluten-free if needed

2 teaspoons baking powder

¼ teaspoon kosher salt

1 large Honeycrisp or Granny Smith apple, peeled, cored, and diced (about 1 cup)

⅓ cup chopped walnuts (optional)

Preheat the oven to 350°F. Line an 8x8-inch metal baking pan with parchment paper, spray with cooking spray, and set aside. (You can use a glass dish if that's what you have, just note that the bars will take longer to bake.)

In the bowl of a stand mixer fitted with the paddle attachment, add the **butter** and **coconut sugar** and beat on medium speed until fluffy, about 3 minutes. Add the **eggs** and **vanilla** and beat on medium speed until just combined, about 1 minute. Add the **flour**, **baking powder**, and **salt** and beat on low speed until just combined, about 1 minute. Remove the bowl from the mixer and fold in the **apples** and **walnuts** (if using). You can also do the mixing with a hand mixer, if desired, and still just fold in the apples and nuts at the end.

Add the mixture to the prepared baking pan and spread in an even layer. Bake until a cake tester or toothpick comes out clean, 35 to 40 minutes. Set the pan on a wire rack to cool completely. Slice and serve.

Store extra blondies in an airtight container in the fridge for up to 5 days, or in the freezer for up to 2 months.

NOT-SO-BASIC BASICS &

STAPLES

Fluffy Quinoa
with a Protein Boost

MAKES ABOUT 3 CUPS

Gluten free
Dairy free
Nut free

1¼ cups chicken stock or bone broth

1 cup white quinoa

Kosher salt and freshly ground black pepper

In a medium saucepan over medium-high heat, add the **stock**, **quinoa**, and **½ cup of water**. Bring to a boil, reduce the heat to low, and cover. Simmer until the quinoa is just tender, or even a little firm in the middle, about 15 minutes. Remove the pan from the heat and let sit, covered, for another 10 minutes.

Fluff the quinoa with a fork, season with **salt** and **pepper** to taste, and serve.

Store any leftovers in an airtight container in the fridge for up to 5 days.

My Tried & True Simple Rice *with a Protein Boost*

MAKES ABOUT 3 CUPS

Gluten free
Dairy free
Nut free

2 tablespoons extra-virgin olive oil

1 cup long-grain white rice

2 cups chicken stock or bone broth

Kosher salt

In a medium saucepan over medium heat, heat the **oil**. Add the **rice** and toast until the rice is fragrant and has absorbed some of the oil, 2 to 3 minutes. Add the **stock** and a pinch of **salt** and bring to a simmer, stirring occasionally. Reduce the heat to low, cover, and simmer until most or all of the liquid has been absorbed and the rice is cooked through, about 20 minutes. Remove the pan from the heat, fluff the rice, and cover for 5 more minutes. Season with more salt if needed and serve hot.

Store leftovers in an airtight container in the fridge for up to 5 days.

2-for-1 Herby Rice

MAKES ABOUT 3 CUPS

Gluten free
Dairy free
Nut free

CILANTRO-LIME RICE

1 teaspoon extra-virgin olive oil

1 cup white basmati rice

1 cup chicken or vegetable stock

Kosher salt

2 tablespoons chopped fresh cilantro leaves

Juice of 1 lime

LEMON-PARSLEY RICE

1 teaspoon extra-virgin olive oil

1 cup white basmati rice

1 cup chicken or vegetable stock

Kosher salt

2 tablespoons chopped fresh parsley leaves

Juice of 1 lemon

In a medium saucepan over medium heat, heat the **oil**. Add the **rice** and cook, stirring frequently, until the rice is fragrant and toasty, about 1 minute. Add the **stock**, **1 cup of water**, and a big pinch of **salt** and bring the rice to a boil. Cover, reduce the heat to low, and cook until the rice is tender and all of the liquid is absorbed, 15 to 20 minutes. Remove the pan from the heat. Stir in the **cilantro/parsley** and the **lime/lemon juice**, fluff the rice with a fork, and cover for 10 more minutes. Serve warm.

My Go-To Japanese Sweet Potato Wedges

SERVES 2 TO 4

Gluten free
Dairy free
Nut free

2 large Japanese sweet potatoes, scrubbed

2 tablespoons avocado oil

Kosher salt and freshly ground black pepper

Preheat the oven to 425°F. Line one large or two standard baking sheets with parchment paper and set aside.

Cut each **sweet potato** in half, and cut each half into 8 wedges. Add the wedges to a large bowl and add the **avocado oil** and a generous amount of **salt** and **pepper**. Toss well to coat.

Spread out the sweet potato wedges on the prepared baking sheet(s) in an even layer, leaving space between each potato wedge. Roast for 20 minutes, flip, and continue cooking until tender inside and crispy outside, 15 to 20 more minutes. Let cool slightly before serving.

No-Fryer-Added French Fries

SERVES 4 TO 6

Gluten free
Dairy free
Nut free

4 medium russet potatoes (about 1½ pounds), scrubbed

3 tablespoons avocado oil

Kosher salt

OPTIONAL SEASONINGS

Smoked paprika

Garlic powder

Freshly ground black pepper

Cut the **potatoes** into roughly ¼-inch-wide sticks and add them to a large bowl. Cover completely with cold water and let soak for at least 30 minutes, or up to overnight in the fridge (cover the bowl if you go this route).

Preheat the oven to 450°F. Line two baking sheets with parchment paper and place them in the oven to preheat.

Drain the potatoes and use a clean kitchen towel or paper towels to dry them thoroughly.

Transfer the potatoes to a large bowl. Add the **avocado oil** and a generous sprinkle of **salt** and toss gently to coat. (The potatoes can be a little tender after their soak, so handle with care!)

Remove the sheet pans from the oven, and carefully (remember, the pans are hot!) arrange the seasoned potatoes in an even layer, spacing them so they're not crowded or touching.

Bake for 15 minutes, until the undersides have begun to brown. Flip the potatoes and bake for another 10 to 12 minutes, until the fries are golden.

While they're still hot, sprinkle the fries with more salt as desired, plus any of the seasonings above (or other seasonings you like!). Serve hot with DIY Ketchup (page 225), Creamy, Pour-It-on-Everything Feta Sauce (page 226), Too-Easy-Not-to-Make Ranch Dressing (page 228), or Honey Mustard Sauce (page 162).

Better than TJ's Ride-or-Die Kale Pesto

FREEZER-FRIENDLY

MAKES ABOUT 1½ CUPS

Gluten free
Dairy free

- 2½ cups roughly chopped Tuscan kale
- 1½ cups lightly packed fresh basil leaves
- ½ cup raw cashews, sunflower seeds, or pine nuts
- ¼ cup extra-virgin olive oil
- 3 garlic cloves, peeled and left whole
- Juice of 1 lemon
- Kosher salt and freshly ground black pepper

In a food processor, add the **kale**, **basil**, **cashews**, **oil**, **garlic**, **lemon juice**, and **salt** and **pepper** to taste and process until smooth. Taste and check for seasoning, and add a splash of oil or water to thin the pesto if desired.

Store in an airtight container in the fridge for up to 1 week, or freeze for up to 2 months.

Better than Fresh, Frozen Broccoli in the Oven

SERVES 4

Gluten free
Nut free

- 1 pound frozen broccoli
- 2 tablespoons extra-virgin olive oil
- ½ teaspoon garlic powder
- Kosher salt and freshly ground black pepper
- Grated Parmesan cheese, for serving (optional)

Preheat the oven to 400°F. Line a baking sheet with parchment paper.

Add the **frozen broccoli** to the prepared baking sheet, spreading it in an even layer to leave a bit of space between the florets. Roast until the water has evaporated, about 10 minutes. Drizzle the broccoli with **olive oil** and season with the **garlic powder**, **salt**, and **pepper**, plus the **Parmesan** (if using). Return the broccoli to the oven and roast until tender and a little browned along the edges, 10 to 15 minutes.

Top with more Parmesan (if desired) and serve warm.

Creamy, Better-than-Store-Bought Hummus

MAKES ABOUT 2 CUPS

Gluten free
Dairy free
Nut free

- 1 (15-ounce) can chickpeas, rinsed and well-drained
- ¼ cup tahini
- 3 tablespoons fresh lemon juice, plus more as needed
- 2 tablespoons cold water, plus more as needed
- 1 tablespoon extra-virgin olive oil, plus more for serving
- 1 garlic clove (or more if you're a garlic lover!)
- ½ teaspoon ground cumin
- Kosher salt
- Ground sumac, for serving (optional)
- Smoked paprika, for serving (optional)

In a food processor, add the **chickpeas**, **tahini**, **lemon juice**, **water**, **oil**, **garlic**, **cumin**, and **salt** to taste. Process until completely smooth and creamy, 4 to 5 minutes (yes, that long!). If the hummus doesn't look quite creamy enough or is too thick, add a bit more cold water and continue processing. Taste and add more salt or lemon juice as needed.

If serving right away, spread the hummus onto a large plate and top with additional oil, plus **sumac** and/or **smoked paprika** if desired. Or transfer the hummus to an airtight container and store in the fridge for up to 1 week.

Simply Perfect Caramelized Onions

Gluten free
Dairy free
Nut free

- 2 tablespoons extra-virgin olive oil
- 3 large sweet onions, thinly sliced
- Kosher salt

In a large skillet over medium heat, heat the **oil**. Add the **onions** and a big pinch of **salt** and cook, stirring frequently, until the onions are translucent and starting to turn golden, 8 to 10 minutes. Reduce the heat to low and partially cover the pan. Continue cooking, stirring occasionally, until the onions have reduced in volume and are a deep, rich brown color, about 45 minutes. Remove the pan from the heat.

Use right away or let cool and store in an airtight container in the fridge for up to 5 days.

DIY Toasted Cracker Breadcrumbs

FREEZER-FRIENDLY

MAKES ABOUT 1 CUP

Gluten-free friendly
Dairy free
Nut-free friendly

3 cups plain or sea salt crackers, gluten-free if needed (I use our cadootz! sea salt crackers, of course)

Kosher salt and freshly ground black pepper

FOR AN ITALIAN VERSION, SEASON WITH THE FOLLOWING BEFORE BAKING

½ teaspoon dried parsley

¼ teaspoon dried oregano

¼ teaspoon garlic powder

¼ teaspoon onion powder

Preheat the oven to 300°F. Line a baking sheet with parchment paper and set aside.

In a food processor, add the **crackers** and **salt** and **pepper** to taste. Process on high speed for 30 seconds for coarse, panko-style breadcrumbs, or 1 minute (or more) for finer breadcrumbs.

Transfer the crumbs to the prepared baking sheet, spreading them in an even layer. Bake until golden and a bit fragrant, 5 to 7 minutes. Set aside to let cool completely.

Transfer the breadcrumbs to an airtight container and store for up to 6 months in a cool, dark cupboard or the fridge. Or store them basically forever in the freezer (no need to thaw before use, since the crumbs are so small they'll thaw on their own within minutes).

Shockingly Easy DIY Ketchup

MAKES ABOUT 1½ CUPS

Gluten free
Dairy free
Nut free

1 small (6-ounce) can tomato paste (about ¾ cup)

¼ cup coconut sugar, plus more as needed

2 tablespoons white vinegar

2 tablespoons apple cider vinegar

1 teaspoon kosher salt, plus more as needed

1 teaspoon onion powder

½ teaspoon garlic powder

In a small saucepan, whisk together the **tomato paste**, **coconut sugar**, **white vinegar**, **apple cider vinegar**, **salt**, **onion powder**, **garlic powder**, and **1 cup of water**. Set the pan over medium-high heat and bring to a simmer. Reduce the heat to low and cook, stirring frequently, until the mixture has thickened slightly, 3 to 5 minutes. Remove the pan from the heat.

Taste and add more salt or coconut sugar as needed. Let cool completely before using.

Store in a jar in the fridge for up to 2 weeks. (This does not last more than a few days at my house!)

Better-than-the-Restaurant Special Sauce

MAKES ABOUT 1 CUP

Gluten free
Dairy free
Nut free

½ cup mayonnaise

¼ cup DIY Ketchup (page 225) or store-bought

2 tablespoons sweet relish

2 teaspoons yellow mustard

1 teaspoon distilled white vinegar

½ teaspoon ground paprika

½ teaspoon garlic powder

½ teaspoon onion powder

Kosher salt

In a medium bowl, whisk together the **mayonnaise**, **ketchup**, **relish**, **mustard**, **vinegar**, **paprika**, **garlic powder**, **onion powder**, and **salt** to taste.

Store in an airtight container in the fridge for up to 2 weeks.

Creamy, Pour-It-on-Everything Feta Sauce

MAKES ABOUT 1 CUP

Gluten free
Nut free

6 ounces feta cheese

⅓ cup milk of choice (dairy or nondairy)

1 tablespoon fresh lemon juice

In a food processor, add the **feta**, **milk**, and **lemon juice** and process until completely smooth.

Store in an airtight container in the refrigerator for up to 1 week.

Delectable Chimichurri Sauce

MAKES ABOUT 1½ CUPS

Gluten free
Dairy free
Nut free

- 1 cup lightly packed fresh parsley leaves
- ½ cup lightly packed fresh cilantro leaves
- 1 medium shallot
- 2 tablespoons white wine vinegar
- 1 garlic clove
- ¼ teaspoon kosher salt
- ¼ teaspoon dried oregano
- ¼ teaspoon smoked paprika
- ⅓ cup extra-virgin olive oil

In a food processor, add the **parsley**, **cilantro**, **shallot**, **vinegar**, **garlic**, **salt**, **oregano**, and **smoked paprika** and pulse until the herbs are very roughly chopped. Add the **oil** and continue pulsing until the mixture has a loose, saucy consistency.

Store in an airtight container in the fridge for up to 5 days.

Too-Easy-Not-to-Make Ranch Dressing

MAKES ABOUT 1½ CUPS

Gluten free
Nut free

- ⅔ cup plain Greek yogurt
- ⅔ cup mayonnaise (or more yogurt, if you're mayo-averse)
- 2 garlic cloves, grated or minced
- 1 tablespoon fresh lemon juice
- 1 tablespoon chopped fresh dill
- 1 tablespoon chopped fresh parsley leaves
- 1 tablespoon chopped fresh chives
- ½ teaspoon garlic powder
- ½ teaspoon onion powder
- Kosher salt and freshly ground black pepper
- Milk of choice (dairy or nondairy) or water, as needed, to thin

In a medium bowl, whisk together the **yogurt**, **mayonnaise**, **garlic**, **lemon juice**, **dill**, **parsley**, **chives**, **garlic powder**, **onion powder**, and **salt** and **pepper** to taste. Add a bit of **milk** or water to thin the mixture if desired. Taste again and adjust seasonings.

Store in a jar in the fridge for up to 10 days. This dressing tastes best after it's had a chance to marinate for a few hours in the fridge.

A Bit Lighter Greek Yogurt Caesar Dressing

MAKES ABOUT 2 CUPS

Gluten free
Nut free

- 1 cup plain Greek yogurt
- 1 cup grated Parmesan cheese
- 4 garlic cloves
- 4 small anchovy fillets (omit if this isn't your thing)
- Juice of 1 lemon
- 2 tablespoons Dijon mustard
- 2 tablespoons extra-virgin olive oil
- Kosher salt and freshly ground black pepper

In a food processor, add the **yogurt**, **Parmesan**, **garlic**, **anchovies** (if using), **lemon juice**, **Dijon**, **oil**, and **salt** and **pepper** to taste. Process until completely smooth. Taste and adjust seasonings as desired.

Store in an airtight jar in the fridge for up to 1 week.

Ginger Sesame Dressing

MAKES ABOUT 1 CUP

Gluten free
Dairy free
Nut free

¼ cup extra-virgin olive oil

3 tablespoons toasted sesame oil

3 tablespoons coconut aminos

3 tablespoons rice vinegar, plus more as needed

1 tablespoons maple syrup

1 tablespoon minced fresh ginger, or ½ tablespoon ground ginger

2 garlic cloves, minced

Kosher salt and freshly ground black pepper

In a medium bowl, whisk together the **olive oil**, **sesame oil**, **coconut aminos**, **rice vinegar**, **maple syrup**, **ginger**, **garlic**, and **salt** and **pepper** to taste. Taste and adjust the seasonings, adding more vinegar or salt as needed.

Store in an airtight jar in the fridge for up to 1 week.

ACKNOWLEGMENTS

Jordan—My forever partner. Thanks for supporting me and my never-ending urge to start a new project. You were my original taste-tester in our 450-square-foot apartment, and you never questioned my crazy idea of sharing recipes on the internet. I love doing this life with you and being on this wild ride together both personally and professionally. Because what's crazier than three kids? Three businesses. I couldn't do it without you. Love you always.

Ezra, Brody + Cooper—My boysssss, my crazies, the absolute loves of my life. I do it all for you three. The brutal honesty from each of you, the crazy preferences, and the endless requests in the kitchen consistently keep me humble and on my toes. You know I will always drop anything for you. Thanks for making every meal an adventure and motivating me every day.

Mom + Dad—My ride-or-dies, my #1 supporters. The groupies at every trade show, every event, every panel, you name it. You never questioned or doubted me for wanting to pursue food content as a career. You always believe in me, you support me, and you know just when to throw fuel on my fire to keep me going. Thanks for being my confidantes, defending me while keeping me grounded, and dropping everything to be there for me always. And thank you for helping however you can so I can continue to pursue my career as a working mom.

Seth—I am the luckiest to have a brother like you. Forever thankful for our relationship and to have you in my life. We may have the most different taste buds, but I will share my milk chocolate gems and chocolate-almond Perfect Bar stash with you any day.

Elissa + Glenn—In-laws like you don't come around too often. Thank you for being a huge support for not only Jordan and me, but also for our boys. I wouldn't be able to do what I do without your extra hands, and I am so appreciative for you both.

Lisa—Where do I even begin? You are my rock. My morning, afternoon, and evening phone call and text. The person I talk to the most outside my family. You truly are my sister, and I am your 4th? 5th? sister, and I'd basically be in a ditch without you. You mean the world to me and have believed in me before I even knew you. Thankful that my career brought you to me and we have truly watched each other grow. There is something so beautiful about that. You are a gem in this world and I cherish our relationship more than you know.

Sarah—Remember when I wanted to write a memoir eight years ago and you candidly told me that was the dumbest thing and that people want food from me and not life lessons from a twenty-seven-year-old? You always have your pulse on everything. I don't know how you keep up with everything, but you are a powerhouse of a human, the ultimate stylist, and I wouldn't be here if it wasn't for you as my hype woman! Thank you for being with me since the really early days.

Justin—I knew when Sarah and I walked into your office this was going to be it. You genuinely care for your authors in a way that challenges them and also turns their books into the best they can be. Thank you for believing in me and my mission with this book and bringing on the mom author you needed in your amazing portfolio. You are a rockstar editor, and I loved getting the live feedback of my recipes at the photoshoot. I hope you enjoyed that freezer stash I sent you home with!

The Simon Element team—Gina Navaroli, Richard Rhorer, Farzana Razak, Jen Wang, Cecilia Gray, and the entire publishing team who helped bring *More, Please!* to life, thank you. I appreciate each and every one of you and your efforts. You were truly the dream team.

Jeanelle—I knew on our first phone call you'd be an absolute pleasure to work with. Peak efficiency is my love language and you mastered that. I loved our phone calls and hearing about your family and neighbors enjoying the recipes in this book. Thank you for making sure each and every recipe coming out of my kitchen is perfect and for helping the queen of typos get her tush in gear for this book.

Lauren Volo—You bring the exact energy every author wants on a photoshoot. The most calm, cool, and collected human. A powerhouse and beyond talented photographer who captured the moments I was looking for in *More, Please!* You are incredible, patient, talented, and I loved working with you for this book. Please answer my call when we do another!

Cyd, Maeve + team—Reunited and it feels so good! Honestly when Lauren said she'd be bringing Cyd for food styling and Maeve for prop styling, it sealed the deal. You guys are amazing and it was an absolute pleasure working with you both again. You and your teams were phenomenal. I still am in awe over Tommy's perfect meatball skills and think of him every single time I try to make them look as good. Thanks for bringing the hustle and making every photo look gorgeously delicious.

INDEX

Note: Page references in italics refer to photos. Freezer-friendly dishes are indicated with asterisks.

G

H

I

J

K

L

M

SIMON ELEMENT

An Imprint of Simon & Schuster, LLC
1230 Avenue of the Americas
New York, NY 10020

Food stylist: Cyd McDowell

Food stylist assistant: Tommy McKiernan

Food stylist assistant: Debbie Kim

Prop stylist assistant: Ashleigh Sarbone

Prop stylist: Maeve Sheridan

Prop stylist assistant: Fabi Arce

Prop stylist assistant: Tsering Dolma

Studio: Blue Salt Studio

First Simon Element hardcover edition August 2026

Interior design by Farzana Razak and Jan Derevjanek

Manufactured in China

10 9 8 7 6 5 4 3 2 1

Library of Congress Control Number: 2025945933

ISBN 978-1-6680-8212-6
ISBN 978-1-6680-8213-3 (ebook)